DATE DUE

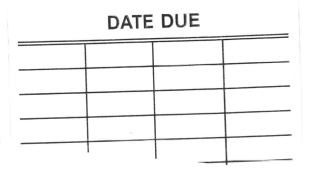

Accountability and the Public Interest in Broadcasting

Also by Andrea Millwood Hargrave

CULTURAL DIVERSITY IN THE POLICY ENVIRONMENT (2005)

HARM AND OFFENCE IN MEDIA CONTENT: A Review of the Evidence (with S. Livingstone, 2006)

Also by Colin Shaw

RETHINKING GOVERNANCE AND ACCOUNTABILITY (BBC Charter Review series, ed., 1993)

DECIDING WHAT WE WATCH: Taste, Decency and Media Ethics in the UK and USA (1999)

Accountability and the Public Interest in Broadcasting

Andrea Millwood Hargrave

and

Colin Shaw

palgrave
macmillan

© Andrea Millwood Hargrave and Colin Shaw 2009

All rights reserved. No reproduction, copy or transmission of this publication may be made without written permission.

No portion of this publication may be reproduced, copied or transmitted save with written permission or in accordance with the provisions of the Copyright, Designs and Patents Act 1988, or under the terms of any licence permitting limited copying issued by the Copyright Licensing Agency, Saffron House, 6-10 Kirby Street, London EC1N 8TS.

Any person who does any unauthorized act in relation to this publication may be liable to criminal prosecution and civil claims for damages.

The authors have asserted their rights to be identified as the authors of this work in accordance with the Copyright, Designs and Patents Act 1988.

First published 2009 by
PALGRAVE MACMILLAN

Palgrave Macmillan in the UK is an imprint of Macmillan Publishers Limited, registered in England, company number 785998, of Houndmills, Basingstoke, Hampshire RG21 6XS.

Palgrave Macmillan in the US is a division of St Martin's Press LLC, 175 Fifth Avenue, New York, NY 10010.

Palgrave Macmillan is the global academic imprint of the above companies and has companies and representatives throughout the world.

Palgrave® and Macmillan® are registered trademarks in the United States, the United Kingdom, Europe and other countries.

ISBN-13: 978–0–230–01920–1 hardback
ISBN-10: 0–230–01920–X hardback

This book is printed on paper suitable for recycling and made from fully managed and sustained forest sources. Logging, pulping and manufacturing processes are expected to conform to the environmental regulations of the country of origin.

A catalogue record for this book is available from the British Library.

Library of Congress Cataloging-in-Publication Data
Millwood Hargrave, Andrea
    Accountability and the public interest in broadcasting / Andrea Millwood Hargrave and Colin Shaw.
        p.   cm.
    Includes index.
    ISBN 978–0–230–01920–1
    1. Broadcasting policy.   2. Broadcasting—Social aspects.   I. Shaw, Colin, 1928–   II. Title.
    PN1990.83.H37 2009
    384.54—dc22   2008035149

10   9   8   7   6   5   4   3   2   1
18   17   16   15   14   13   12   11   10   09

Transferred to digital printing in 2009.

Contents

Preface

The profusion of economic and technological changes which has marked the past 40 years provided the background against which we came to write the book, a collaborative venture in every respect. We had been colleagues at the short-lived Broadcasting Standards Council, inaugurated in Britain in 1988 and incorporated into the new Office of Communications (Ofcom) 12 years later. Although initially suspected as a tool for further intervention in broadcasting by an interventionist government, the Council's role was advisory and, generously funded, it was able to develop fresh areas of research as well as providing an independent assessment by lay persons of a range of complaints about broadcast programmes on radio and television. Questions of accountability and the public interest recurred frequently in the daily work of the Council and its staff. Both concepts are elusive, varying at different times between and within societies. We therefore wished to explore them further.

In expressing our first set of thanks to the British Academy for funding our research, we should say that it was following a proposal from the Academy that we widened the scope of our enquiries to countries overseas. We chose Australia, India and the US, all of them, it was pointed out, democracies. We considered whether we should substitute one of those three countries for a country with less democratic structures and less developed civil societies. However, it seemed to us that a single country of that kind could hardly stand as an example of a large variety of others and that to make a second substitution of the same kind would diminish the value of the original project.

Nobody writing about broadcasting in three of the countries studied can omit expressions of gratitude to Asa Briggs for his *History of Broadcasting in the United Kingdom*, Eric Barnouw for his comparable volumes on US broadcasting and K.S. Inglis for his histories of the Australian Broadcasting Corporation (ABC). There were other authors, too numerous to mention, who frequently stimulated and challenged our thinking before and during the writing of the book. We were looking for contemporary interpretations of the concepts rather than examining the scholarship of the past. The main weight of our research rested on a long series of interviews whose individual length was customarily an hour. Thanks to the generosity of the Academy, we were able to carry out interviews in 2007 personally in India and the United States (US), as well as in the United Kingdom (UK). In Australia, the interviews were undertaken by Julie Eisenberg, to whom we owe a profound thank-you for the diligence with which she administered our questions, developed valuable supplementaries and responded to queries up to the completion of our work.

In all four countries, our interviewees included broadcasting managers, commercial and public, policy makers, regulators and academics, some in retirement, but mostly active. Not all of them could be quoted in the book and some, when quoted, appear with undeserved brevity. Without exception, however, they contributed greatly to our understanding of the issues we raised. Some we already knew and sometimes had worked with, others we sought out at the suggestion of colleagues and friends. We are especially grateful to all those who agreed to be interviewed and for their willingness to give so generously of their time and experience. Where they have been quoted, they have been given the titles of their posts at the time of the interview. The imperfections which remain are of our own manufacture.

Paul Honey, then attached to the Oxford University Programme in Comparative Media Law & Policy, detailed for us the governing instruments and institutions in the four countries and the legal frameworks in which they worked. We owe him many thanks for this valuable body of research. Our thanks are also due to the BBC's Written Archives Centre at Caversham, where the staff were, as always, attentive and helpful during our visit.

We are particularly grateful to Steven Barnett, David Oswell and Michael Starks for their helpful and instructive comments.

Finally we would like to express our thanks to our respective families for their support and forbearance. Without them, our labours would have been more laborious and much less personally rewarding.

1
Introduction

*I think fundamentally that there is a tension between accountabil-
ity and the public interest. It's fundamentally between what people
want and what people need. It's society making judgements about
the latter, the (BBC)Trust regulating them.*
(Richard Hooper, former Deputy Chair, Ofcom, UK)

In the middle years of the last century, from the late 1920s to the end
of the 1980s, it all appeared fairly straightforward. International agreements involving up to 200 countries provided each of them with a share
of spectrum, an allocation of frequencies which it was the individual
nation's right to deploy as it pleased, provided that it did not interfere
with its neighbours. Arrangements differed within states: commercial
operations in one place, state-dominated monopolies in another, a mixture of the two somewhere else. No less a variety of revenue streams
provided the funding: state grants, licence-fees, advertising and subscription. And across the globe broadcasters operated under licences
from the state with varying degrees of oversight of performances and
of enforcement.

All this began to unravel in the 1980s. Change, when it came, came
two-pronged. One was economic, the other technological. Their conjunction was to precipitate a revolution which affected many aspects of
the national and individual lives. To take the former first, the growing dominance of free market economics throughout much of the
world has been a feature of the past five decades. At one extreme,
it reflected a cardinal belief that the market, left to itself as the
expression of countless individual decisions, would self-regulate. It
was a period when, in many parts of the Western world, there was
a turning away from Big Government which was often perceived as

1

intervening unnecessarily or incompetently. It threatened enterprise and, in seeking to direct and control, generated overweighty bureaucracies. Deregulation, adopting 'choice' as its watchword, was the goal many governments now set themselves. There was money in abundance to underwrite the new entrepreneurial culture as it searched out fresh fields which it could conquer and, where it had to, compete ferociously.

The second, technological, prong was the development of digitalisation. Put at its simplest, digitalisation allows the broadcast signal to be converted into code and then compressed. One consequence is a marked improvement in the quality of the signal. More far-reaching in its consequences, however, is the release of many new frequencies, producing a substantial increase in the number of channels available for broadcasting, abolishing the constraints which had underpinned the case for regulating a scarce resource. We are told that spectrum scarcity is only temporarily at an end, but for the moment the way is open for the launch of a very large number of enterprises. Many of them are far removed from the conventional models of broadcasting which characterised much of the last century.

The coincidence of these two changes has produced a situation which raises questions about the nature of the broadcasters' accountability: to the legislature and the government, to one or other or both. Many of them, however, now have a prime accountability to their shareholders and would acknowledge that they have no less accountability to the publics they serve. And it has also been said, even formally prescribed, that they have obligations to the public interest.

It was against this background, driven by our experience and interest, that we conceived of this project. It was not intended to be a review of the academic, or even industry, literature on what 'accountability' means, or has come to mean. The project was not designed to offer a conceptually based definition of 'the public interest'. Rather, it was designed to test how relevant the concepts of accountability and the public interest remain in broadcasting and in the newer forms of delivery of media content. Thus, the project explores the views and attitudes of those working in the communications industry (although the emphasis is on broadcasting, particularly in Australia and India) and those that are observers of it (either because of their current position or because of their former employment). The project is also able to offer a comparison between four relatively different broadcasting and media environments, with differing industry, regulatory and legal structures and, importantly, different cultural starting points.

The original title of the book was to have been *The Public Interest and Accountability*, but we realised early on in the interviews, the backbone of our work, that accountability provided an easier starting point for our discussions. Initially, it is a matter of accounting for money received and spent, only thereafter do other issues arise and lead on to the public interest, a concept altogether more fugitive. When we put our questions in reverse order, leading with accountability, we found the results more substantial.

We believed, however, that, in the drive for one kind of accountability, the sort that comes from calculation and measurement, our societies stood in danger of losing sight of all those other things which broadcasting can bring: the insights, the knowledge, the challenges to eye and ear, the influences which are not susceptible to measurement, but can be one of the greatest rewards for those who look or listen or, in these days, interconnect. Those to whom we talked were, we hope, representative of both approaches: endorsement of the market and scepticism about its ability to realise all those possibilities.

Set against these considerations is the relentless advance of technological change which, it is thought by some, challenges the very structures of social cohesion that broadcasting supports while others – also interviewed here – argue that the social contract is not broken but changed. Certainly, the Internet, while not yet universally available in all the countries considered here but significant in each, offers a delivery medium that crosses all societal sectors and contributes not just culturally and socially, but has major economic impact. The debates reflected here raise crucial questions for each of the four free societies we have discussed.

2
Accountability

Accountability and what it means

The study found no single definition of accountability for organisations within the broadcasting and communications fields but many variables which constituted elements of accountability that depended on other components such as the range of stakeholders involved, funding and so on. There is a definition of accountability that comes from another field (that of humanitarian aid) which says it goes beyond reporting on decisions and actions but looks to take

> account of the needs, concerns, capacities and dispositions of affected parties, and explaining the meaning and implications of, and the reasons for, actions and decisions. Accountability is thus a measure of the quality of the relationship between an agent (a body offering a service or product) and a principal (the person or group for whom the service or product is intended).[1]

While coming from another area, this relationship between parties involved as agent and principal can well be applied to broadcasting.

Certainly, for most interviewees, attempts at a definition led to conversations about structures and processes. Richard Hooper, formerly Chair of the Radio Authority and former Deputy Chair, Ofcom, UK, warned of the consequences of the lack of a definition:

> I think that the word 'accountability' is abused and misused and used by everybody and nobody seems to ever define it very much. Talking about mantras, it becomes a mantra and people then start splitting hairs and saying, well, it's something called answerability. I think it's quite a difficult word.

4

A number of interviewees drew a distinction between the accountability of publicly supported broadcasting organisations which had either direct funding or some other public benefit given to them (such as spectrum access), and commercial institutions (which had to satisfy the needs of shareholders, for example). Steven Barnett, Professor of Communications in the Department of Journalism and Mass Communications at Westminster University in the UK, explained:

> Accountability in the Public Sector is about the expenditure of public money. So how do you and I and other people out there who are paying taxes or licence-fees or whatever to a public body or the government elected by us, how are they accounting to the people who pay those taxes for what they do in terms of the transparency of actions, in terms of efficiency, in terms of their definitions of what constitutes the appropriate way of spending that money, outcomes, gains, losses, etcetera? And I do think it's different because in the corporate world there are things like corporate social responsibility and there are things like your carbon footprint and there are public goods and public losses. But in the end it is about accountability to shareholders, that is your only legal obligation, actually, and anything beyond that is out of the goodness of your corporate hearts.

For Michael Grade, Executive Chairman of ITV plc, a commercial public service broadcaster in the UK, there were three groups of stakeholders to whom ITV was accountable and the support of the last two was dependent on his organisation being able to provide the first, the audience:

> Three people: the audience, the paymasters the advertisers and the shareholders. And you have to find areas where, sufficient areas where, those three interests converge so that you have actually got a business at the end of the day.

This connection with, and dependence on, the audience to achieve the desired business models was heard time and again during the interviews, especially where a directly commercial relationship was required (based on subscriptions or advertising). It created a very real and critical relationship between the broadcaster or communications platform and the user:

> Special interest groups and people outside of our business often miss a fundamental, economic fact. That is, commercial broadcasters

compete with each other every minute of every day for viewers. And if they don't have local content that is relevant and of interest to those communities, viewers simply switch the channel and go to where they can find it. That is absolutely the way our competitive business works. Growing the viewer base enables the operator to meet shareholders' expectations. If viewers are not watching, and the operator can't sell the advertising inventory, the shareholders won't support the operator over time. That's the way the business model works.

(Marcellus Alexander, Executive Vice-President of Television, National Association of Broadcasters, US)

However this direct relationship with the user or audience was not important just to the commercial organisations. Publicly funded institutions, such as the Australian Broadcasting Corporation (ABC) in Australia, are clear that their accountability is to their viewers and listeners:

Our principal accountability is to ensure that we are providing services that are valued by all Australians.

(Murray Green, Director of Corporate Strategy and Governance, ABC, Australia)

Mark Thompson, Director-General of the BBC in the UK, acknowledged that the public lies at the centre of a group of 'institutions and structures' to which his organisation is accountable; that is, they have a democratic mandate:

I think the public are sovereign. In other words, all accountability avenues lead to the public in the BBC. But we would certainly recognise that the people have a number of representative institutions and civic structures which we also need to have regard to. We need to have regard to them because they represent the public in different ways. And obviously Parliament and the government are critical to that. They are chosen by the public to represent their interests. The public pay a licence-fee directly to the BBC, in respect of our services. Their money comes to us, we can deliver our services directly to them . . . unlike some other public service broadcasters around the world, part of our status is to have this direct line to the public.

As this chapter will go on to show, processes and mechanisms are key to how organisations – and those observing from the outside – feel they are held accountable, but some interviewees, while demanding clarity, argued against rigidity. For example, Jean Seaton, Professor of Communications and Media History at the University of Westminster in the UK, argues that accountability allows those providing broadcasting services to work within understood parameters, although the parameters themselves might be fluid and should be allowed a certain latitude as developments occur. Here, she was talking about the processes of accountability between the BBC Executive and the governing body which regulates it , the BBC Trust, and the inflexibility they might generate:

> Nor do I think that you ever get accountability actually by pinning things down...I don't see that any of the mechanisms it's [BBC] got make it more accountable...because (the Trust has) got no powers over the only things that matter which is kind of a negotiated relationship to programmes. I cannot see how you can have the kind of discussions you need to have and give the broadcasters the kind of support they need: It's kind of support, warning, it's carrots-and-sticks.

The special place of broadcasting

> The media industry is a different industry in some ways because of its social, cultural and political effects.... It's an industry with a particular impact on public life that's different from other industries – transport or banking.
>
> (Professor Andrew Kenyon, Director, Centre for Media and Communications Law, Melbourne Law School, Australia)

Those interviewees who work within broadcasting felt strongly that their industry is different from other industries. As the comment by Andrew Kenyon above shows, this is because of a conviction that broadcasting has a special place in the social, cultural and economic fabric of a country. Accordingly their levels of accountability are, in many ways, greater. The way in which these influences were described by interviewees is discussed further in Chapter 3.

Those who work within public service broadcasting (PSB) – people interviewed included those from the ABC in Australia, the BBC in the UK, Prasar Bharati in India and a public service broadcaster, WETA, serving the Washington DC area in the US – have an even stronger sense of the responsibility placed upon them because of the nature of their organisation. For Paul Chadwick, Director of Editorial Policies at the ABC in Australia, the notion of influence upon the public and society meant that a key component of his industry – to reveal information – requires his organisation to be able to stand up to scrutiny itself. This is more marked, he argued, now than ever before:

> We are a media entity, we engage in scrutiny and disclosure of other institutions and quite rightly we do that about government etc and we're doing it more about ourselves and that's partly what my job's about. I think more and more the old media institutions – that is, those from the pre-Internet days, established newspapers, established broadcasters – will have to attend to these questions of quality assurance, accountability, transparency, much more carefully than they did in the past.

Uniquely among the countries surveyed for this project, the public service broadcaster in India, Prasar Bharati, is aware of its particular role as a driver for social change in the country, reaching rural as well as urban communities (see section 'India' in Chapter 4 for further detail of the broadcasting environment):

> In Prasar Bharati, our objective and focus have been more or less the same. We have social concerns. We have concerns of information you know and we have a mandate for trying to be a catalyst for social change so all those duties are still with us as a public broadcaster.
>
> (Ashok Jailkhani, Deputy Director-General, Doordarshan, India[2])

As suggested above, part of the public service broadcaster's heightened sense of accountability comes from the particular way in which it is supported (financially or otherwise) by government and, in some cases, directly from the public purse. In the US the Public Broadcasting Service (PBS) has some government funding but the public service broadcasters also receive financial pledges from viewers and listeners, which further increases their sense of accountability to the audience. Michael Getler, the independent Ombudsman appointed by the PBS, explained,

> [PBS] gets a portion of its funding, about 15 percent, from the Congress, through Congressional appropriations. But they get the largest part of their funding from contributions from viewers. So, when people object or question something that's on public

television, it's not like they're writing a letter to the New York Times or an email to ABC or NBC or something like that. They are saying, "my tax dollars support you and how dare you present such and such a programme". In other words, even though a relatively small amount of taxpayer funding goes to PBS, it gives viewers a pretty big weapon to use against them when they don't like something. It is more frequently introduced as the basis for criticism than is the individual contribution.

On the other hand, Tim Gardam, Principal of St Anne's College in the University of Oxford in the UK, suggests that technology has removed some of the 'specialness' of broadcasting. The increased accessibility of media content through the freeing up of spectrum through digitalisation, and the affordability of domestic reception devices, has meant that broadcasting's particular place of social and cultural influence is being eroded. Information and key events, for example, formerly only available through the broadcast medium, are now more available generally:

We have seen a move from a historic belief that broadcasting was somehow inherently different from other forms of media towards a recognition that, with the revolutionary changes in digital technology, the nature of that difference is changing with it, quite substantially so.

The suggestion that technology may diminish the importance of broadcasting is not always accepted. Indeed, some argued that broadcasting, and the issues that derive from it, is very particular. As Rakesh Kacker, former Adviser to the Telecommunications Regulatory Authority of India (TRAI), described when he was talking about the possible formation of an independent communications regulator in India,

TRAI had proposed that there should be a converged regulator for carriage issues and a separate regulator for content. The argument being that the kind of intellectual input that you require for content regulation is very different from carriage. For content regulation you require some sensibility about society's tastes and differences, artists who understand these issues whereas carriage, it tends to be about technology, and economics and that kind of thing. The two functions are totally different and they require totally different intellectual inputs and expertise.

The tension created by trying to regulate two different targets – broadcasting or broadcasting-like content, and telecommunications – was raised also by Georgina Born, Professor of Sociology, Anthropology and Music at Cambridge University in the UK. She argued that the creation of a converged regulator in the UK does not necessarily overcome nor meet with the particular difficulties raised by converging technologies but simply re-configures how they are addressed:

> This bizarre attempt [by Ofcom] to say that economic and market issues can be entirely separated from content, quality and programme issues seems to me very problematic. (It) shows particularly when you're looking at TV production issues – for example when you have evidence, from independent research, which raises questions of declining quality, repetitive programming and lack of innovation, but you can't bring the thinking together.... I do think that what you see in Ofcom is a very elaborate attempt to transcend and circumvent the criticisms of the earlier structure of broadcasting in the country, whether it was the Governors of the Beeb [BBC] or the IBA [the Independent Broadcasting Authority]; this whole critique of an elite-capture, sort of middle-class values, Establishment, a set of judgements or rulings in this industry. But the problem is that this separation of the cultural and the economic and this huge overloading of economists in Ofcom – it doesn't solve anything; it just remixes it and separates it out in a new way.

Levels of accountability

There are different arrangements in place to allow for accountability, and the national studies describe these in some detail. This chapter considers more broadly how these systems are implemented within organisations and how external factors impact on participants within the broadcasting and other media industries.

Interviewees were able to respond to questions about the particular arrangements both within their organisations and those imposed upon them from without. They understood that their internal structures are open increasingly to scrutiny from outside. Importantly the issue of accountability was not restricted to media organisations alone, those producing or transmitting programmes and other content, but it spread in many interviewees' minds to the regulators and other guardians of the industry. Bill Buzenberg, Executive Director of the Center for Public

Integrity who worked previously for National Public Radio in the US, said,

> I think accountability is a word we really like, along with trans-
> parency. This means public accountability to us. We all can under-
> stand that governments or publicly held corporations should be
> accountable. To me, the Federal Communications Commission (FCC)
> is accountable to the public. I think what's happened lately is we've
> short circuited that accountability to the point where the FCC is
> mostly accountable to special interests, not the public interest.

The first point of accountability within organisations lies with the way in which senior appointments are made. In particular, the independence or otherwise from the government of the most senior staff was felt to be key to ensuring accountability. In India for example, there is resistance by the commercial broadcasters to planned moves for statutory inde-pendent broadcasting regulation – much of the argument is based on the fact that the Board appointments to the proposed broadcasting regulator would be government-led and thus are not perceived as independent of government. Indeed many of the senior staff currently working for the public service broadcasters and communications regulators in India are former civil servants.

> There have been some concerns expressed by the people, various
> associations, broadcasters, that the way it is proposed that it may
> not be able to be totally independent. Because the appointment pro-
> cess proposed (will) be by the Central Government. Therefore, there
> should be some Central Committee, so that it ensures that the right
> kind of people come in, not only the people which the Government
> wants to come in, they should be representing a diverse section of
> the society who are really concerned for the sector. That is the issue
> which we are trying to address now. How to make it more indepen-
> dent, both functionally and financially, and the appointments.
> (Arvind Kumar, Director (BP&L), Ministry of
> Information and Broadcasting (MIB), India)

In the US, the Chair of the FCC – the industry regulator – is directly designated by the President and the Board of Commissioners is made up of representatives, by and large, from the two major political parties – the Republicans and the Democrats. While this gives rise to criticisms of political capture in some quarters, there was another argument, voiced more than once, that politically elected representatives have the right to act as agents for the public at large:

> The Chair [of the FCC] is particularly political because the Chair is always designated by the President [all members are nominated by the President and confirmed by the Senate]. Even though he can only have three representatives from the same party, the Chair doesn't automatically go across when there's an election. It could be viewed as a problem area or it could be viewed as a fundamental approach to accountability.
>
> (Monroe Price, Director, The Center for
> Global Communication Studies at the Annenberg School
> for Communication, University of Pennsylvania, US)

In Australia the Chairmen of the ABC and Special Broadcasting Service (SBS) are appointed by the Governor-General, the representative of the Queen and, as such, have no current political affiliations. In the UK, the Chair and Board Members of the regulatory authority, Ofcom, are ministerial appointments, following the observance of formal principles prescribed for public appointments.

Procedures for accountability within organisations provide for transparency within the decision-making process – 'transparency' being an oft-used word which is, itself, an element of accountability.

> Our processes there are to engage with the regulator and to make submissions, which are usually public submissions, so people can see what we're saying, and to engage with government of course about our views on the same issues. And to hope that we're able to achieve a reasonable outcome. That's the first line.
>
> (Bridget Fair, Manager of Regulatory and Business
> Affairs, Seven Network, Australia)

As suggested, transparency is one of the principles mentioned by a number of interviewees when talking about accountability – by this they mean the ability for the processes to be examined in some detail. Reed Hundt, former Chair of the FCC, said,

> The enemy of change that serves most people is the structure of control that currently exists and that enemy has one tool that is powerful above all, and that is the cloak of secrecy. So all that enemy needs to do is drape the cloak of secrecy over the issue and then public

opinion cannot form. Because public opinion says "I don't know what's going on".

Concern was voiced in some quarters that the procedures were not followed appropriately at all times. In the aftermath of the Hutton Inquiry in the UK in 2004, there was particular criticism of the governance arrangements of the BBC.[3] One of the most serious concerned the relationship between the Board of Governors, first installed in 1927, and the Executive Board of Management.

> In the current world [2004, the BBC] didn't have the separation that was required to persuade other people that the BBC wasn't doing just whatever it wanted and taking no notice of anybody else, to put it crudely.
>
> (Andrew Ramsay, Director-General, Creativity, Culture and Economy, Department for Culture, Media and Sport, UK)

In Australia for example, a new role – that of Director of Editorial Policies – has been created within the public service broadcaster, the Australian Broadcasting Corporation (ABC), so that internal procedures may be followed and there is a redress mechanism in the event of failure. The person in this role is Paul Chadwick (see above). To overcome any possible mistrust of his work he made sure that he visited the ABC's various offices upon taking up his post, both as means of introduction but also in recognition of the potential for fallibility among staff who are themselves sometimes subject to uncertainties. There is a clear recognition that many of the systems in place actually help people within organisations by providing a framework, or a rule, against which one can check one's actions, not necessarily in a judgmental manner. Paul Chadwick insisted that this is done for other industries where the public interest or even public safety is significant, and so it should be done for broadcasting.

> If you develop those fair and rigorous methodologies and you take an honest look at your performance you can get better, it can be good for you. Other businesses do it all the time. The creators of foodstuffs have to do it in order not to poison people. And the creators of motor vehicles have to in order not to put unsafe products on the market. Although journalism is not directly comparable to those two industries, there are things you can do to see whether you are upholding the high standards you set for yourself and if you're not, there are

things you can do to get better. And I think that kind of work is worthwhile, not just in and of itself, but because it builds the public trust and credibility.

For Martin Le Jeune, Director of the consultancy, Open Road, and former Head of Public Affairs at British Sky Broadcasting (BSkyB), the satellite and new media broadcaster in the UK, it is obvious that the organisation has to keep abreast of the mood of the audience and the industry in order to stay ahead in the marketplace and keep both the audience and – by extrapolation – the shareholders satisfied:

> Sky is built on two very solid foundations. One is commitment to customer service: to keep customers, build a relationship with them, market services to them that they will buy and value – so the company needs to keep that tiptop. Second is the return to shareholders which we have been pretty effective on. If we can manage to make those two things reinforce one another then we have an arch to go on those foundations – the strongest form of architecture you can have. Other audiences, other stakeholder groups and so on, I see those as developing from the strength of those two.

While those interviewed from both the publicly-funded and the commercial institutions saw their primary role is to satisfy their audiences and users, the object of their accountability was different. Those who receive public subsidy had to satisfy those who give them funds or other benefits that the resources are well spent, frequently to further some 'public good'. The commercial sector must answer to its shareholders. This led to different requirements in the way accountability was thought of.

Within many of the organisations from which interviewees were drawn, there are systems that allow interaction and response to feed back into the organisation at some senior level. In the UK, the regulator Ofcom has a wholly independent board, the Consumer Panel, which considers consumers' interests. In Australia the ABC and the SBS both have advisory bodies, recruited to consider interests within the community and, as it was described to us, to act as 'a bit of a sounding board for contentious issues'. The independence of these bodies from the main Boards, while situated within the overall framework of the organisations they assist, means that they are able to raise issues of concern, bringing a different perspective based on their own areas of expertise. In the UK for example, the Consumer Panel has championed and pushed forward issues such as access of the new technologies for disabled people, placing challenges before both the regulator and the industry.

Co- and self-regulation

This chapter, and this project, was not designed to look at types of regulatory structure in any detail. Nonetheless, it was clear that co- and self-regulation were, for some interviewees, forms of accountability. This was particularly true in the commercial sector where statutory regulation has less purchase. In Australia, each sector within the television industry is required to develop its own codes of practice. The publicly funded National Broadcasters have to inform the regulator, the Australian Communications and Media Authority (ACMA), of their codes, but do not need its approval. The commercial broadcasters must agree their codes with the ACMA in return for a limited amount of statutory oversight. With this come some additional requirements such as the need to have an effective complaints handling system in place, and to provide adequate consumer information:

> One of the obligations was that we took over our own complaints handling and the regulator only steps in when there are unresolved complaints. We also have to give the consumer information about what they are about to see. So it's not only the [ratings] symbol which comes up at the start of a programme ... we also have to say 'In addition to the above, the following programme is classified – for example 'M'; it may contain drug references, it may contain violence etc'. So it's about public awareness as a quid pro quo for developing our own codes.
>
> (Debra Richards, Chief Executive Officer, Australian Subscription Radio and Television Association (ASTRA), Australia)

In India the commercial or private broadcasters have codes of practice for use within their own organisations. Sagarika Ghose, a news anchor at CNN-IBN (an independent news channel in India), who also runs a highly successful blog, says the service she is involved with prides itself on not sensationalising events, but on bringing 'difficult' stories to the public's notice, relying on self-restraint and internal governance procedures:

> There is very little accountability that is exercised outside the organization, we exercise our own accountability. We have a code written out and we follow that.

The Indian government is trying currently to impose a statutory broadcasting code and is being resisted by the industry. In turn, various sectors of the industry, such as news services and entertainment channels, have developed genre-specific codes. The News Broadcasters Association (NBA), formed in 2007, has, at the time of writing, submitted to the government for approval two codes. One covers journalistic ethics and broadcasting standards (such as the maintenance of objectivity and impartiality in reporting) and the other offers mechanisms for a dispute resolution system. This debate has not come to a close (see Chapter 4 for more information).

Editorial policy

Systems exist in a number of broadcasting organisations allowing the internal processes to feed into editorial policy. Sometimes this feedback came from the audience:

> Our view at Seven [an Australian commercial television channel] is that it's best for people who are directly involved in programme making to have a very clear and direct view of what concerns there are in the community, because it's one way of making sure that programs meet community needs. Whilst that's a very grandiose statement, meeting community needs means making programs that people want to watch and that means getting good ratings and that means driving advertising dollars, so it's a very important part of our operation.
> (Bridget Fair, Seven Network, Australia)

These areas of public engagement will be considered in more detail later but what is important is the aspiration within organisations that programme creators should understand what the public's sentiments are. This was mirrored in the comment by the PBS Ombudsman, Michael Getler, who runs a public Internet-based column as well as writing for a PBS staff audience:

> the problem with this job is, you know, you have to be critical in order to do it properly and when you are critical people inside don't usually come over and say, "gee thanks". So you never know what goes on after a column appears exactly. But I think people – inside PBS and the stations and the independent producers – read it and they think about it, and think even more about what they are doing,

and that's sort of the most you can do. I can't force them to do anything. But I can put pressure on them, and push them to think about
it more the next time.

Public engagement: Consultations, research and complaints

Consultations

When describing the importance of public input into issues concerning
the broadcasting industry, Jock Given, professor of Media and Communications at Swinburne Institute of Social Research in Australia,
highlighted the fact that certain key issues may not become part of
the public agenda until a bigger question is raised. Referring to the
debate about media ownership in Australia, it was not until the government sought to change the media ownership rules that the debate
about the place of local news and information in broadcasting was
raised.

I think as far as the possibility for public input:

- it shows that, first, official regulatory processes, official policy makers
  (were) slow to attend to an issue that was of more public importance
  than they acknowledged or realised;
- it highlighted the fact that the time when things happen is often
  when there is some larger policy deal being done and something gets
  done about a small point which has struggled to get itself on the
  public agenda;
- but thirdly, it highlights the fact that even with public concern, the
  seriousness of the issue can be dwarfed by wider considerations.

Throughout the project this was a constant refrain – external, often commercial, pressures are thought to be applied, frequently to the detriment
of a more general and public good.

Mark Armstrong, Director of Network Insight in Australia, former
Chair of the ABC Board, also talked at some length about the assumption that the public temperature was being taken through the use
of consultation and research and argued for the time when physical
submissions were made to the regulator.

The effect of engagement and real contribution happened when people had the right to appear to follow up on a submission or, in cases
of individual radio stations in rural areas, simply to appear. In all my

experience with law and broadcasting I've never found any substitute for the eyeball experience. Despite technology, the only way we know we will be heard is if we have eyeball contact with the decision makers.

His view stood almost alone, however, and most interviewees talked of different forms of research and public consultations (often distributed now via the Internet) as the way in which the public or social mood was examined. Here Penny Young, Head of Audiences at the BBC Trust in the UK, talked of the way in which the Trust operates to allow participation by those interested in particular decisions.

Nowadays, it's important in accountability terms to be open to everybody. So the Trust has to be clear about when the [BBC] Trust window is open to say "right now we're thinking about this decision, here's the information, and here are the options we're choosing between and so on. We'll let you know about our consultations; we'll listen to everyone; and we'll consider the arguments on merits".

As the UK national study will show, both the BBC Trust and Ofcom, the regulator, use public consultations and research extensively to demonstrate their accountability to their various stakeholders. There was cynicism expressed by some interviewees about how independent and fair public consultations were. They questioned how fully responses were assessed, and whether there was not sometimes an element of cherry-picking in order to support decisions already made.

The legislation, quite dishonestly, describes processes that have to be written, as public processes or a favourite form of public inquiry in Australian communications, not just broadcasting, a public inquiry is everybody is given the right to make submissions to the Department of Communications or the Minister about a topic. Now I've been in many situations where the decision makers never read the submissions.

(Mark Armstrong, Network Insight, Australia)

There were also some criticisms of what was called the 'modern accountability route'. Consultations were not always thought to be the best way, as both Given and Armstrong above suggest, of gauging what is truly in the minds of society at large. Further, there was the question about how active the public was, or wanted to be, in matters of broadcasting. There was an argument that the issues that seemed important to commentators on the industry – as distinct from the industry itself – did not really make the public feel strongly. Some argued that there are cultural issues at play, as suggested by Lyn Maddock, Deputy Chair of the regulator, the ACMA:

> I think that in some ways one of the characteristics of the Australian community is – it's often called tolerance, sometimes it's called apathy – is that there is a capacity to actually not bother about what you don't think is very important.

Other interviewees had a much more direct way to gauge public opinion or the way in which audiences were reacting – the ratings or, the case of American public service broadcasters, the amount of funding they received from the public. Here Mary Stewart, Vice-President of Communications at WETA in Washington, likens the direct funding her organisation gets with the feedback loop in the theatre:

> I came from a theatre background and you could go down to the theatre during the performance and hear the applause – or not. Here we have an odd thing called "pledge drives" where people call you up on the phone voluntarily because you've gone on the air and asked them to do so. They tell you whether they like the show or not and how much they're going to support you. It is a very vitalizing and empowering thing for the audience in many ways.

Indeed, any direct interaction was generally thought important by the interviewees as it allowed the broadcaster to engage with the audience or user:

> What Schedule 2 of the BSA [Broadcasting Services Act] adds is a broad expectation that members of the community served will have the opportunity to participate in both the operations and the programming decisions of the service and that provides an important guarantee that it is media for the people by the people, to use that kind of hackneyed phrase.
>
> (Barry Melville, General Manager, Community
> Broadcasters Association of Australia)

> We have enough things that we do on the air which asks for citizens' opinions, ask them to send us reports, ask them to write to us, email us, send us a video, dial into us, talk to them on the street,

there is enough so-called consumer interest interface. I wouldn't call it activism but interface.

> (Sunil Lulla, CEO, Times Now (a commercial
> television news channel), India)

This call to action, described by Sunil Lulla, was significant for many of those interviewed – and technology had made this interplay between broadcaster and audience or user far easier than before, through the use of email and other forms of electronic communication.

Research among the public

For most interviewees nonetheless, market and social research was the vehicle used to learn what it is that concerns the public. This research was described variously, and different methodologies were employed, but it was felt by many to support decision-making or to allow the organisation to understand what it is that the audience and other stakeholders, such as industry, are concerned with.

> There is certainly accountability back to the community because you need those subscribers because if you don't have a subscriber, you don't have a business. And so you do constant research into what do they think of the service, what do they think of the price, that sort of thing, so that is ongoing, you know. And you use audience research for programming and scheduling.
>
> (Debra Richards, ASTRA, Australia)

For the UK regulator, Ofcom, research plays a significant role:

> Research is critical because that is how we understand the views of citizen-consumers in the UK and of industry so I would think we believe very strongly as an evidence-based regulator that research plays a critical role in looking at trends and then understanding issues and understanding public perception of issues and what's important to the public. And then I would say that the nature of the research that we do, we tailor the research that we do to kind of make it fit the purpose, depending on the particular issue that we have at hand ... we try and stay at the cutting-edge of what is available and what is appropriate from a research perspective to ensure that we're always best in class in terms of what we do and the evidence that we bring back to help inform our thinking and our regulatory policy in this area.
>
> (Helen Normoyle, Director of Research, Ofcom, UK)

Ofcom not only conducts research among the public but also undertakes research among those it is required to regulate, its 'clients' in industry and other associated bodies, that might have an impact on the work of Ofcom, or be impacted by it.[4]

Research can also be used as an effective counter to calls for decisions to be made that would not necessarily be supported by other groups, including, sometimes, the public. It is here that policy makers have to make decisions based on factors which go beyond the specific issue at stake and elements of the 'public interest' come into play. Lyn Maddock of ACMA described how research was used to justify the regulator's decision in the face of political opposition over an issue about broadcasting content standards in Australia:

> What is public opinion? If you take what our surveys, focus groups, and complaints have shown the mass of the populace thinks, then we were pretty much in touch with what they were thinking. If you take it as to what those who comment in public wanted, we were often seen as out of touch, but we made sure at the time of our review that we did quality research, we did general surveys, we had focus groups, we looked at ratings and we had the legitimate complaints to us. And I think most people weren't concerned.

The compulsion to 'mechanise' or quantify many aspects of broadcasting has led the industry to find different ways to represent the audience. Television viewing and radio listening figures (audience ratings) are common to all the countries examined. In all the countries, apart from India, there is also a move to quantify other elements. The most recent and clear example of this is the BBC's adoption of a Public Value Framework which uses a mixture of criteria, including the six Public Purposes set out in its Royal Charter (see Chapter 3 for a description of the Purposes) and market impact assessments, to predict the effect of its broadcasting or other activities on the public and the market (for example, making programmes available on demand through the BBC iPlayer after their transmission). This attempt to find such measures, outside the use of ratings data, was much debated in the build-up to the formation of the BBC Trust. The Controller of Public Policy at the BBC, David Levy, warned against a 'single size suits all' approach:

> I think all of this comes back to the mood of the times, a view that you need to be able to quantify much better to demonstrate the value of what you're delivering in public services more generally. Of course

there are limitations to how far you can go, but that's what we're trying to do in trying to introduce a comprehensive, but simpler over-arching framework that applies to everything the BBC does, rather than multiple different measurement frameworks.

Similarly, an Australian public service broadcaster pointed out how difficult it was to argue, numerically, for certain benefits over and above others, when making a bid for investment, especially with public money:

> The quantitative stuff is straightforward – it's more demanding find-ing significant indicators of output that indicate that there is a reason for public investment here and there is public value and public good deriving from that investment.
>
> (Murray Green, ABC, Australia)

As noted, all the countries considered in this project collected ratings data to help programme makers gauge the popularity or otherwise of their programmes. Some broadcasters also use other, more qualitative, indices tracked over time. For example, how much audiences 'appre-ciated' the programme across a number of variables such as interest, perceived quality of programming, originality and innovation. On the back of this, advertising and other means of evaluating success were argued for.

Peter Lunt, Professor in the School of Social Sciences and Law, Brunel University, in the UK, suggested that caution needed to be used in the interpretation of data. In most research, the commissioner of the research is dictating what work should be undertaken. Peter Lunt stressed that research should not be managed so that the 'correct' answers could be arrived at and argued that the originators of research should be held accountable themselves, and that their processes should be transparent.

> At least with research, you've gone out and you've talked to people, and you've got some amount of diverse public opinion represented, and of course it's a distillation, it's a summary that's all. And it's crit-ical who has control over that because they can claim accountability in the face of the public, but it's more a traditional notion of account-ability to the public, which treats the public as a relatively passive court.

Sonia Livingstone, Professor of Social Psychology in the Department of Media and Communications at the LSE in the UK, agreed with this, adding that the public must be allowed to have a voice in debates:

[Research is] done by either the industry or the regulators on behalf of the public, and there are real issues as to how far the researchers are accountable.... For the public to be accountable they have to speak and they can either speak through research or through some sort of civil society organisation, and these get positioned as biased in various ways, which they may be, and research is not normally transparent enough to read. So how is the public to hold the BBC, or anyone, to account?

Other forms of research were used extensively to support decision-making.

Grievances

Complaints handling has become a bit of serious political issue recently. I'm not sure it's a serious community issue.
(Bridget Fair, Seven Network, Australia)

As well as research, complaints or the notification of grievances were a way in which organisations felt they were able to respond to their accountability remit. The role of complaints and the processes by which complaints were handled were important. Most of the organisations had harnessed technology and complaints generally could be made via email or by phone. Almost all had internal complaints systems and some, such as the PBS with its independent Ombudsman, had additional layers of independent advice or recourse available.

I think the job for most people when they want to complain is to work out who to complain to and I know that because a lot of people think they come to us and we get a lot of calls about that. Most people do probably think they go first to the broadcaster and can then take their complaint somewhere else. I mean, all of those things are documented and publicised and I presume ACMA deals with them reasonably well, but I think it is in the nature of most people not to complain.
(Jenny Buckland, CEO, The Australian
Children's Television Foundation)

Most of the interviewees discussed the 'traditional' ways in which public or user grievances were treated – so they talked about the structures they have put in place. The capture of the complaints process by special interest groups was not much mentioned. This was true despite the potential for abuse created by the ease of access to the complaints procedures via the newer technologies, such as email. This interviewee was the only one who mentioned a difficulty with 'organised' complaints:

> We find the people who write to MIB [Ministry of Information and Broadcasting] are three kinds of complainants. Some are malintent, designed to be an irritant. Some are political and some are genuine. They are led by public interest legislation or NGOs or public advocacy groups.
>
> (Sunil Lulla, Times Now, India)

The information derived from complaints is used not only internally by the organisations affected but externally by commentators as a way in which to judge the 'health' of the organisation being examined:

> The complaints process I think has improved a good deal. We get much more information now about decisions that have been made and that's to do with the use of the internet and the fact that this is now the jurisprudence of complaints. (It) is very important for broadcasters to see those decisions made about complaints that get escalated to the regulator, to actually know what that means.
>
> (Jock Given, Swinburne Institute of Social Research, Australia)

> That kind of curiosity about whether people are satisfied with your complaints handling once a period of time has passed by is a good curiosity to have.
>
> (Paul Chadwick, ABC, Australia)

External accountability

The way in which organisations found themselves accountable to external bodies formed a key part of this research. It was clear that regulators played an important role in the broadcasting industry and the role of the government was also closely examined. This research did not dwell on accountability to shareholders by commercial entities, as this was felt to be a given. Nor did the project dwell on the way in which shareholders and advertisers might affect (directly or indirectly) the practices of a broadcaster. However, an implicit consideration of these was apparent in the concerns raised by some interviewees about the concentration of media ownership and consequent lack of pluralism (an issue current in the US at the time of interviewing).

Regulation

Within this project, India was alone in having no independent regulator to oversee broadcasting content issues (see Chapter 4 for more information). The responsibility for such matters there currently sits within MIB, although an independent broadcasting regulator has been proposed. In the three other countries an independent (converged) regulator examines broadcasting issues. In each of these countries, the regulator is considered to be accountable primarily to the parliamentary system, through which accountability to the public is maintained. This echoes the argument above that, although appointments may be based on political favour, they could be seen to be reasonable insofar as those making the appointments have themselves been elected by the general public, the electorate. This view was proffered in the US where such a system is well-entrenched. For example, when asked to whom the regulator was accountable, a Washington DC Broadcast Attorney said,

Two places. Obviously the Congress, Congress controls the purse strings. I'd say probably first Congress and then also the Executive because the Commissioners are appointed by the President and the party that controls the White House gets to control the majority of the Commissioners and they appoint the Chair... they're an independent agency, their accountability to the public is... through the party that gets put in the White House.

In India, on the other hand, the proposed broadcasting regulator has been criticised as being potentially too closely aligned with the government:

But the concept of autonomy is not that well understood in this country and I am sure you will find that regulatory authorities that have been appointed by the government will be looking over their shoulders.

(Sir Mark Tully, Former India Correspondent, BBC, India)

In India and the US then, accountability to the parliamentary process was described as strong. Similarly in Australia, the regulator must go before Parliament triennially to argue for its budget. In the UK however, this relationship was not seen to be as robust. Bill Bush, who had been Adviser to the Culture Secretary at the time of the Communications Act 2003, said,

> Ofcom's accountability to government exists, but it's weak. Its accountability to Parliament, if it even exists, is even weaker.

There were also concerns expressed that the regulator is not always 'heard' by government, especially if government is pursuing its own line of argument or desired policy:

> The dangerous thing is that [Select Committees] can bring out a report and the government doesn't have to take any notice. And that has happened frequently. The government will pick and choose what suits its own policy.
>
> (Jocelyn Hay, Chair, Voice of the Listener and Viewer, UK)

Far more common among the interviewees, especially in the UK, was a question about the evaluation of regulatory decisions and of being able to see how the regulator was coming to its conclusions. A few of the interviewees asked how the regulator could be made more transparent either in their decision-making or, importantly, in any evaluation of their efficacy.

> As far as they are concerned they've done their research, they have passed their accountability test. It does the job they wanted it to do according to their free market agenda and no one asks any questions so they get away with it. Now there's no one, no organisation, no institution, which can look at that and say this has to pass through some kind of test.
>
> (Steven Barnett, University of Westminster, UK)

This was echoed by Robin Foster, former Partner, Strategy and Market Development at Ofcom in the UK and an independent adviser and member of the UK government's Convergence Think Tank (2008):

> For every public organisation there should be some form of external accountability which I'm not sure is in place for Ofcom yet.

And indeed one of the things which I would be very interested in is how that would be designed so that Ofcom would feel, and outsiders would feel, that those various decisions that it had made had been scrutinised fairly and independently.

On the other hand, Monroe Price in the US considered that the FCC had become more accountable because it had to justify its actions in the court and was increasingly using research and other consultative approaches, as Ofcom does, to explain its arguments:

At any rate the one function of the court has been, in theory, to make the FCC more like Ofcom purports to be, an evidence-based policy decision-making authority. And you could argue that it's designed to make it less political, but it may also be because the court, to the extent that it's conservative, thinks that there's no evidence for very much regulation so that the more you are required to justify a regulation, the less regulation there'll be.

Importantly Monroe Price argued that needing to make such justifications may also mean that the regulator is given less leeway. In these circumstances, 'regulatory efficiency' becomes a wall against various sorts of public interest initiatives.

During the interviews in the UK there was much debate about particular incidents that were felt to be failures of regulation (see Chapter 4 for more information). In discussing the need to prevent such incidents, Bill Bush thought that government should play a role. He called for a 'modulated' approach by government which would allow for an early warning when things were going wrong:

What you want, rather than a tipped accountability scale, is something which is much more level. Which feels like an engagement. If things are really going wrong at a strategic level, government can quite properly indicate that they feel they are going off beam. And that modulation is lacking from the system. The nuclear option is available, but the sort of intervention that is greater than tactical but less than nuclear, is not available. [Government] should not intervene at a tactical level, but somewhere between the two there ought to be scope for a hand on the tiller "Are you going in the right direction, is the overall framework about right ?" And that's lacking.

The powers that have been given to regulators were also discussed by interviewees. In the UK the use of sanctions, often financial, seemed to be applied more rigorously than in any of the other countries considered:

> I think penalties are one of the strongest areas of difference between the UK and Australia in terms of media regulation. Ofcom, and the ITC [former commercial broadcasting regulator, now merged into Ofcom] before it, have imposed significant penalties, particularly financial penalties in relation to breaches of their relevant codes and regulations. The approach in Australia in comparison has been far less dramatic.
>
> (Andrew Kenyon, Centre for Media and
> Communications Law, Australia)

The requirement for the regulator to take account of all considerations impartially is, of course, important but there were clear indications – from all the countries – that the power of the industry was substantial. The industry's influence may be through direct action such as lobbying but was more likely often to be a consideration of variables which included the economic health of the country. All the countries involved in this project see communications and communications technologies as the way forward for the fiscal health and development of their societies. Some of the interviewees spoke about this, especially if they themselves were involved in commercial activities. Regulators were not thought of as being in the pockets of the industry, their commitment to being guardians of culture and their obligations to the societies they serve were accepted, generally, by most commentators. However there were some criticisms of the differential way in which they applied their rules and regulations. For example, all the countries have different rules that apply to free-to-air broadcasting, cable and satellite and so on. Part of this is due to the historical fact of the indirect subsidy through gifted or cheaper spectrum for public service broadcasters. Many of the industry representatives interviewed questioned these variable regulations now that other media competitors in the marketplace were vying for the same audience:

> And I think you will find that an awful lot of broadcasters take great pride in the service they give to their communities and don't really have any problem with the public interest obligations that exist. They do certainly have issues, a number of our members, with some of

the economic regulations such as the ownership restrictions, because again these are regulations that apply only to broadcasters and not to our competitors. While they may have seemed much more rational decades ago when they were instituted, to do this in the time when broadcasters are trying to compete against multi-channel competitors and internet-based media, the idea that you have to have structural ownership regulations for the broadcasters, but not on any of our competitors, is a real issue for a lot of our members. So a lot of our members, given today's competitive realities and how they are very dedicated to the best product and serving their community's licence and are very involved in their communities, the differential regulation does bother them a lot.

(Washington DC Broadcast Attorney, US)

This was underscored by Michael Grade of ITV plc in the UK and former Chair of the BBC as its governance passed from a Board of Governors to the BBC Trust:

The biggest challenge we face is the regulatory hangover from the past which still throttles our ability, strangles our ability to be nimble and meet the competitive challenge that we face with Google and who knows who else, and at the same time to get the return to our shareholders. We have to win the battle and the regulator has to face the reality of the economic challenges we face.

When asked about the competence of the regulators to look forward, some concern was expressed about the level of expertise in the areas where regulatory decisions are being taken. In India, the news broadcasters have combined to form their own organisation, the News Broadcasters Association (NBA), to try and fend off increased state intervention (as they see it), arguing for the specialisation of their industry and their readiness to take responsibility for it. The appointment of those with experience of the industry to Boards or within regulators is felt, by some, to engender trust and confidence within the industry. This, in turn, is considered beneficial to the community at large. Michael Grade had overseen the appointment of individuals with practical experience of broadcasting to the BBC Board of Governors.

First time in the history of the BBC that they actually had practitioners on the Board of Governors and on the Trust. I think that's very helpful, I think it gives the Executive confidence that their problems are being understood by people who have been there and done it.

This determination to take responsibility for regulation was evident in many of the interviews conducted. Some reference has been made to the procedures within organisations that lead to what is effectively self-regulation.

> I think it's an element of maintaining public trust that the media be more open about its frailties and its attempts to self-regulate. I also think that if you are not serious about your self-regulation you are at risk of having much more onerous statutory regulation imposed on you. That's not good for freedom of expression generally. In the end it doesn't serve the public. I would much prefer to see the Australian media very serious about its self-regulation and more open about it and it's one of the reasons why I do this job.
>
> (Paul Chadwick, ABC, Australia)

For the Press, self-regulation is the norm, supported by arguments for freedom of expression, increasingly heard in broadcasting. Tim Toulmin, Director of the British Press Complaints Commission (PCC), a non-statutory body with members, both lay and professional, appointed by an independent commission, described the importance of self-regulation for the industry, and the importance of what he called the 'buy-in' from the industry, working with the self-regulatory process:

> If the PCC is to work, it has to have respect from the industry. It's got to have distance from the industry, but it's got to command the respect of it. If we were saying ridiculous things, they simply would not comply with what we were saying. So that means a dialogue with them.

In fact some commentators talked about what they saw as an increasing reliance on co- and self-regulation as forms of accountability, but always within a legal framework.

> There's some literature which I find very appealing in the area of law and economics which talks about responsive regulation. The basic idea is that at the end of the day the law isn't much good, because it's like the nuclear deterrent. You have to have some great big stick in

the background which you hope never to use. The idea of 'responsive regulation' is that you want a richer spectrum of responses. What you want are all sorts of soft in-betweeny things.

(Dr Andrew Graham, Master, Balliol College,
Oxford University, UK)

The effect of such 'responsive regulation' would perhaps not be so different from current regulation, it was suggested, but would shift responsibility to other players in certain areas:

There's a general widespread trend towards that anyway. . . . politically over the last 20 to 30 years, there's been a trend towards forms of self and co-regulation and I think in digital communications it is particularly appealing. It is almost like there will be a set of layers – there will be an element that is directly controlled and other elements that aren't. . . . But the effect in the end I'm not sure is that different from what we've had before. Its effect on industry might be less but it's trying to find a way to deal with the content through a mix of a set of processes, a system, a code of practice in place to deal with them and some link back in appropriate areas with traditional areas of either criminal or traditional regulation.

(Andrew Kenyon, Centre for Media and
Communications Law, Australia)

The roles of government and parliament

From many of the interviews, and as mentioned above, it was clear that the role of the national parliament – elected representatives of society – is becoming more significant. Some interviewees cautioned, however, against the risk of capture of the political process by interest groups, rather than the government acting as a 'voice of the people' more generally:

You only need enough people to get you into the Senate, and for the Senate to be balanced in a particular way, which gives you a much stronger voice than your community representation, for those views to hold sway.

(Bridget Fair, Seven Network, Australia)

I guess one question would be, are there areas in which Congress is a surrogate for some sort of 'popular spirit'. So in the standards area, Congress seems to be a surrogate, not necessarily for business but for something else. The FCC on its own wouldn't impose penalties on certain kind of programming, wouldn't be so preoccupied with moral standards, even to the extent it is. It acts because of pressure from Congress which is pressured by constituents. So I guess the question is to what extent are constituents a factor in the FCC's decision making? On the other hand, if you looked at Congress as being a shield for a bunch of forces coming in to define communications policy, then you could argue, and you should argue, that businesses are more important in terms of affecting the entity to which the FCC is accountable, namely Congress, and therefore the Commission is going to be more responsive to their interests.

(Monroe Price, Annenberg School, Philadelphia, US)

In India, it is governmental and parliamentary intervention that has delayed the introduction of a number of bills that would affect the broadcasting and communications industries. In the UK the Select Committees in both Houses of Parliament are playing significant roles in addressing issues of communications generally: The committees each consist of about 12 backbench Members of Parliament under a chairman chosen from either the governing or opposition parties.

If they want to use it for political grandstanding, they will and the kind of issues that crop up in front of committees are very seldom the worthy and dull issues, they tend to be the excitable and exaggerated issues. I think... what the regulator does is to give politicians the opportunity to sound off about stuff... I think politicians have a pulse on what the popular issues are. It's very difficult sometimes as a regulator to keep in touch with that. So appearing in front of a public committee where they do roast you for the sort of stuff which is being talked (about) down the pub is quite a salutary experience when you spend most of your time worrying about next generation access. So the regulator gives them the opportunity to do that and to do it safely and to do it in a way which will be heard, but not in a way that necessarily requires them to take any decisions. The regulator can soak it up, take it in as one of the things they have to take into account, and then make their decisions appropriately. It's a way of allowing the pressure to be there, but not allowing it to dominate.

(Tim Suter, Partner, Content and Standards, Ofcom, UK)

You've got extremely high levels of sensitivity about the relationships between Ofcom and the Government and that independence really has to be protected. In a sense the Select Committee asks the questions and having some light shed on the work of Ofcom by an institution like the Parliamentary Committee would be more effective.

(Damian Tambini, Senior Lecturer,
London School of Economics, UK)

One of the benefits of Select Committees and other such parliamentary devices was that they could uncover evidence not otherwise available. This was felt by many of the interviewees to be important:

It seems to me that they are useful as a way of getting to information which would not be in the public domain if it were not for their role.

(Tony Prosser, Professor of Public Law, Bristol University, UK)

However this role and its perceived benefit – that such committees act as a forum for laying out evidence – was questioned by Jean Seaton of the University of Westminster who argued for better powers to be given to Ofcom to obviate a need for additional scrutiny:

What can the Select Committee do, except call people in and ask questions? Ofcom ought to have powers to do something before you get to a crisis, shouldn't it?

Others argued that the influence of government could have a chilling effect on parts of the industry:

I think we complain about the regulator's work in Australia whereas I think the underlying problem has been for a long time that the ABC never feels particularly loved by government. So it never really has the confidence to go out and draw tough lines in the sand because it is conscious that particularly television networks and radio networks will simply go behind its back and government will do whatever is within its power to essentially run the regulatory process itself.

(Jock Given, Swinburne Institute of Social Research, Australia)

Generally, the role of the government in accountability was accepted.

Government with all its flaws is accountable in a series of ways and provided it doesn't abuse that, it's better to have government accountability. As well as all the other forms, it's not instead of, it's as well as, but the others work better if there is a government backstop.

(Bill Bush, Former Special Adviser to the Culture Secretary, UK)

But some interviewees felt there to be flaws in the governmental process, and there was an insistence that the evidence for any governmental intervention should be clearly marked.

The issue of the way in which governments made appointments to regulators has already been discussed in terms of the regulator's independence. This was a particularly live issue in India where all senior appointees in the public service broadcasters were former civil servants. Their independence from government was questioned by many:

Doordarshan is not independent of government and is not independent of revenue considerations.

(Narayan Rao, CEO, NDTV (commercial news channel), India)

But it was not just an issue in India; in Australia too, the broadcasters tried to ensure that the politicians were kept away from their particular area:

At the baseline, you obviously can't accept that Ministers have any role in dictating what programming should be there and we obviously have a statutory independence in that regard and certain obligations to maintain that independence and despite the pressure over the years that has come on us from various sectors of the community, we've always tried to resist that.

(Bruce Meagher, Special Broadcasting Service, Australia)

Our principal accountability is in terms of reporting annually to the Parliament which we do. We also appear three times a year before the Senate in the Senate Estimates process which ostensibly is designed to look at how Commonwealth entities spend public money. I think some of the Senators take a very broad view of that accountability and want to engage on editorial matters, which they certainly do. And we do that two or three times a year.

(Murray Green, ABC, Australia)

There was some criticism of the way in which certain parliamentary processes were run. Andrew Kenyon of the Centre for Media and Communications Law spoke about the Australian experience:

The biggest legislative changes that involved parliamentary committees considering possible change and calling for public submissions and producing a report in the last couple of years, changes relevant directly to media and to things like the IP [intellectual property] and copyright issues and the Australia–US Fair Trade Agreement, happened with an opportunity for public input but within incredibly limited time frames, and probably increasingly so. And therefore there was a limited sense that 'we' even mattered. I know a number of academics for example, who wouldn't want to take part in such a process.... They think 'this is silly, this is not proper consultation, why should I even give it the appearance of validity?'

In Washington, the role of lobbyists and powerful constituents, such as industry, came up in a conversation with Rick Chessen, Adviser to Commissioner Copps of the FCC in the US:

There are certainly Washington lobbyists who call the FCC regularly and probably get more information about what's going on here in the scheduling and when to come in for meetings. Face-to-face meetings are very important. It's not like the Department of Justice, or say the Federal Trade Commission where, I understand, they meet less often with members of the public. This is a very permeable place where, in addition to the paper record, we have meeting after meeting with people who come in and personally argue their case. So if you have somebody in Washington who knows when an item is going to be considered you obviously have the advantage of coming in and making your case before the Commissioners. Especially if you know when it is what we call 'on the 8th Floor', when an item is up for a decision and you can come in at the moment the decision-makers are actually looking at it and focussed. It makes a difference.

Marcellus Alexander noted the importance of local political involvement to the members of his organisation, the National Association of Broadcasters:

If, while managing local television stations, a member of Congress comes home for recess, or just happens to be in town...or if the General Manager is here in Washington DC, they should make certain their Senator or representative is briefed on the good work the station is doing. Whether it's reporting on at-risk, vulnerable communities, or what is being done to help education in classrooms, operators should let them know the initiatives being undertaken to serve their community. That way, when there's a piece of legislation coming up that might be detrimental to the broadcast business, the Congressional members understand that business. Perhaps they say: "Wait a minute. These guys are good folks in the community. They are doing work that matters and are making a difference. We cannot let that legislation happen because it will negatively impact their stations and they may not be able to do some of the things the community needs".

While there is a debate in the UK about the importance of 'localness' in radio, Bill Bush thought this was an area that television should stay out of. Newer media delivery platforms were better suited to such content, he argued that:

There is absolutely no indication that people want to be active in that space except through what you might call the YouTube or FaceBook kind of "Here's our garden fence, isn't it fantastic?". They're going to bypass TV completely and go straight into downloading onto web-sites. The BBC shouldn't be there, very expensive, not sure what it offers. I don't think people want it, I think they want something very informal in that space and user-generated content is very suited for super-local media.

In contrast to this view about local media, regional differences were recognised as important in Australia, India and in the UK. In Australia the indigenous communities are provided for, while in India the public service broadcaster must cater to the regional markets through local pro-gramming and language. In the UK there are channels providing Welsh and Gaelic programming, while the regulator has created Boards repre-senting each of the four nations of the UK. The tension between the desire for national cohesion in the UK on the one hand, and broadcast-ing's role in that, and devolution on the other hand, is discussed further in Chapter 3.

Advocacy groups

If the government should be seen as the elected representatives of the public, advocacy groups were seen as the mouthpiece of certain factions within society.

First, it depends a great deal on who's running the show. Second, there are strong institutional biases in favour of the regulated entities. We refer to this in the literature as regulatory capture. So, while steps are taken to try and create some public accountability and access, the system is not very user friendly for the public, which is exactly why groups like mine exist.

(Andrew Schwartzman, President and
CEO, Media Access Project, US)

Advocacy groups as a way of bringing issues to notice that would otherwise be ignored were used widely in the US, but were also seen as inefficient by some:

[The issue of debt in the US] just falls between the cracks. This serious issue is never on the agenda, it's never really dealt with fully in the press. It's also not dealt with by this administration which prefers to simply ignore it. Congress would just as soon ignore it, too. With such avoidance, bingo, you have a serious dollar situation. You have serious imbalances. You have a lot of things happening, simply because this issue of the debt hasn't been addressed. If you're relying on advocacy groups to address it, that simply won't happen.

(Bill Buzenberg, Center for Public Integrity, US)

We've got a million intermediary groups, it's not like we have any shortage of intermediary groups. Some of them are less powerful than you might think they would be or that maybe you think they should be but we've got lots of them and any given American who's even modestly active in society is probably the member of more than half a dozen intermediary groups that takes some decision at the FCC.

(Reed Hundt, formerly FCC, US)

In fact funding and the resourcing of such groups was a key issue. In India one such organisation which makes public service documentaries complained about both the inadequacy of its funding and the power of industry:

Civil society groups such as us who are working in this area don't have the resources, don't have the funding to proactively further these [social] agendas and even begin to counter the pressures and the efficiency of industry to be able to influence Government. The other dimension is of course that, because of the other things that are happening to media such as cross media holding and the power of individual media groups and organisations to influence Government, individual politicians tend to be reluctant to take on industry and its agendas.

(Rajiv Mehrotra, Managing Trustee, Public
Service Broadcasting Trust, India)

Nevertheless in India, interest groups were being brought to the table in discussions about the forthcoming broadcasting legislation. But the interests represented by these groups must be properly balanced, and some interviewees warned against capture by special interests:

And I think there's still this question of what's the authenticity of groups that purport to represent segments of the public. Where do they get their legitimacy? Are they just self appointed?

(Monroe Price, Annenberg School, Philadelphia, US)

In the UK the concept of the advocacy group was less well-established, and caution was urged against the use of public outrage as a prompt to action:

I think that the BBC ought to have to respond to strong public opinion, but they ought to respond through some formal institutions. The BBC should not be swept away by any gust of public opinion.

(Lord Rees Mogg, Former Vice-Chair of the BBC, UK)

Although Chapter 3 will consider blogs and their role in the dissemination of information, it was noticeable that blogs were used frequently in the same way as advocacy groups – as a way of urging change or lobbying for a particular position.

Interviewees, when asked, did not consider generally that the press acted as a test for accountability, making broadcasting and other related institutions justify their actions. Certainly the media do look at the media but not in as much detail as might be expected – there was rather less navel-gazing, but what there is was thought to be discerning in its nature.

What I've noticed is that the media's own coverage of media has grown . . . it was an example of what I call the new transparency. What I mean by that phrase is that in the past although the media claimed, quite rightly, that part of its mission was to hold power to account, by exposure and disclosure, it wasn't very good at that itself. I think one of the interesting new phenomena is the way that in cyberspace, the traditional media are being held up to scrutiny.

(Paul Chadwick, ABC, Australia)

None of the interviewees working within broadcasting and other media organisations considered the criticism, sometimes levelled at organisations owned by conglomerates, that their editorial independence might be compromised. However, the concern about such influence was implicit in comments made by observers of the industry about the effect of the potential amalgamation of media organisations and the consequent concentration of media ownership.

The future and accountability

As noted at the start of this chapter, the use of public resources such as spectrum was held to be important enough to require regulation and in turn, a clear system of accountability. These concerns for the appropriate use of such assets remain as concerns for the future and are voiced in different ways in the countries visited. In India an argument is made for public or community access to what is still considered a public resource:

> These are very serious implications for our democracy. While on the one hand we have been pleading for public access, pleading for a certain bandwidth whether it is satellite DTH [direct to home] or whether it is cable, whatever it is, certain bandwidth must be reserved for public access. And there should be an authority that manages public access. Just like the print media liberated the flow of ideas and now with user created content dominating spaces, we must have mechanisms for dissemination until the internet sufficiently penetrates India. We must build this into all our systems and all our mechanisms. That has come up against a complete blank wall. Nobody wants to understand it, nobody wants to listen or even respond to this idea.
>
> (Rajiv Mehrotra, PSBT, India)

In the US there is recognition of the potentially unlimited possibilities offered by the new technologies and a consequent understanding that the way in which they might be managed for the public's good is not yet known:

> Internet technology, and all that it represents, is a destabilising revolution that is well underway and we don't yet know how it's going to

come out. But this fast-paced change is fascinating to me to watch. We can all see big money coming in and trying to buy up Internet properties that are working so these large companies can be more in control of what is happening. But so far, an awful lot of this effort is like the wild wild West in our terms, still out of control. Again, this is a moment which is really interesting and I think this is a great thing that is happening and we don't quite see how it's going to all work out.

(Bill Buzenberg, Center for Public Integrity, US)

In Australia the need for regulation in this area was also referred to:

I'm far from convinced that this era of scarcity has been replaced by the era of abundance, that we have moved beyond an environment where access to particular resources continues to matter. We've only got to look at what's happening with the possible release of vacated analogue spectrum to know that there are particular bits of the spectrum that are more valuable than other bits and that although we might talk about swathes of spectrum being made available, when we actually come to see how much spectrum people need to provide some of the sorts of services that people might be wanting it turns out that we don't get infinity – we get a limited array of services. It may be much less limited than it has been in the past but it's not unlimited. . . . the extent that the most attractive resources are scarce and will continue to be, delivers to me a rationale for continuing to impose some kinds of obligations.

(Jock Given, Swinburne Institute of Social Research, Australia)

This was echoed in the UK:

First of all, anything that makes its way into new media backed by public resources of any sort, a public interest dimension including accountability absolutely has to be part of it. The idea that the sort of Silicon Valley, California circa 1999 free-for-all mentality applies to those sorts of resources is just ridiculous and wrong and it won't last, it won't stick . . . So I think it won't be an immediate thing, but I think as we run up to digital switchover, as we run up through the years of steadily increasing consumption of broadcasting images in those environments, the argument for a regulatory underpinning in those environments will become overwhelming.

(Bill Bush, Former Special Adviser to the Culture Secretary, UK)

Each of these commentators above – only one of whom is directly involved with and working in the industry – argues that regulation will be required even in an age of apparent abundance of media accessibility and media content. But it is the way in which the reins of accountability are held that is going to be increasingly important. Some of the interviewees felt that it was all right to legislate within an unknown environment. Rick Chessen at the FCC commented that the FCC recognised the need for change as new technologies emerge and, while some regulation will be required to provide accountability to users and the industry and other stakeholders, the application of that regulation and the processes involved will change:

> There was a sense that we should think about reducing our reliance on prescriptive rules-based policies in favour of simple rules coupled with strong enforcement of the rules on the books.

This was amplified by Tony Prosser:

> If it's a type of medium which does try to create expectations of trust, then you will have greater duties in response to that, I think, so stronger regulatory requirements. Enforcement will depend on technology.

But a Washington DC Broadcast Attorney queried whether the legislation surrounding the regulatory remit could support the needs of the new communications environment:

> And it still has the handicap of the law and the 1996 [Telecommunications] Act. It's that you have regulatory silos with different kinds of industries having completely different regulatory regimes, with very little in common. You have the telephone companies and traditional common carriers over here, with one set of regulatory regimes, you have broadcasters here, you've got cable operators and multi-channel providers here, then you've got the wild and woolly world of the Internet, not regulated but rolling out here, having great impact on all the others. Unfortunately the law is written and the FCC has to enforce (it) and the FCC's structure still has great difficulty dealing with not only technological change, but convergence.

Others urge caution and argue that more needs to be known about usage and consumer or audience behaviour before decisions are taken.

The issue with new media really is there are two issues that are difficult in terms of the [BBC's] public value test. The first one is that management are trying to predict the future. We are saying we think our predicted reach and share for this service is X and that can only be a prediction. But that's the first problem, because of the uncertainty of predicting the future in a new and unknown market. The other question really is, it's an area where technology changes very fast and the public value test is quite an elaborate, highly structured process and obviously there's the criticism that it moves too slowly to deal with fast changing technologies.

(David Levy, BBC, UK)

Media content providers themselves recognise that they must adapt to meet the coming technologies and most are already doing so:

We now see ourselves as a content provider and that content swims around on different platforms. So that's increasingly the emphasis on how we're conducting our business. We've always been cross platform, we've always done radio and television, we've had a very strong publishing business, both of magazines and books, so now in an integrated sort of way when projects are now being formulated, that cross platform emphasis is right at the beginning rather than something (where) a book comes out of a TV programme at the end or a CD comes out of radio concerts – it's all now done at the very beginning rather than done as an incremental thing as part of the production process.

(Murray Green, ABC, Australia)

This is one of the principal reasons behind the debate, active in each of the countries (bar India), about moving towards increasing self- and co-regulation, rather than statutory regulation. The evolving media delivery platforms require audiences and users to take a far more active role in the way they approach new media content than they do for broadcasting, with its linear programming, delivered in carefully managed schedules. But Robin Foster warns against thinking that the audiences and users can switch to such decision-making processes quickly:

If we are moving to a system where the public are making more choices then it may be that it takes them some time to understand how to make those choices properly in which case you have to find ways of taking them to that final destination.

One of the most important ways in which many countries (including, but going beyond, the four considered here) are encouraging audiences and users to get to *'that final destination'* is by an increasing emphasis on media literacy. This is variously described but Livingstone and Millwood Hargrave conclude that it should include the ability to access, analyse, critically evaluate and create media messages.[5]

Tim Suter acknowledges that self- and co-regulation may be the way forward but argues that some form of statutory regulation may still be called for by society:

> Clearly self-reporting will have a role, but I am not sure that society will quite buy the notion that self-reporting is enough. Now what balance of regulatory and statutory action will end up occupying that middle sphere I don't know, but I suspect that we haven't got an answer on that yet.

Notes

1. http://www.hapinternational.org/
2. Doordarshan is the television arm of the public service broadcaster, Prasar Bharati. The radio arm is All India Radio.
3. The Inquiry was set up in 2003 to establish the circumstances of the death of a British Government scientist. A part of the Inquiry was concerned with the BBC's handling of the episode, which had been heavily criticised by the Government. In his 2004 report, Lord Hutton expressed criticisms of some of the BBC's procedures. The BBC's Chair and Director General resigned shortly afterwards.
4. Ofcom Stakeholder Survey 2007, http://www.ofcom.org.uk/about/accoun/ stakeholder07/
5. http://ec.europa.eu/avpolicy/media_literacy/docs/contributions/68_88_ lmnopqr/68_17_lon_uk.pdf

3
The Public Interest in Broadcasting

Some definitions

My view is that the public interest is the common good, assessed in context.

(Paul Chadwick, ABC, Australia)

Public interest is national interest – they are interchangeable. But there are very subtle variances, certain issues which you may think are national interest issues concerning our foreign policy.

(Ashok Jailkhani, Doordarshan, India)

The concept of the public interest is a battle ground between the right and the left. The left thinks it has real and important meaning. The right usually thinks its invocation is just a mask for the politics of liberal special interest groups. And, according to the right, the only real public interest is the summation of the private interests of all the individuals as embodied in the market.

(Ed Baker, Professor, Annenberg School of Communications, University of Pennsylvania, US)

Public Service Broadcasting defines a relatively small number of broadcasters who do quite big things in a relatively constrained and legally-prescribed way. The public interest is presumably much broader and can be served by a whole load of people who will contribute to the public interest in ways which are far beyond those which are exercised by Public Service Broadcasters.

(Tim Suter, Ofcom, UK)

These four quotations illustrate the breadth of opinions about the public interest in broadcasting which emerge from the four countries under study. They range from, at one extreme, Baker's scepticism, typical of many Americans, about the very existence of such a concept, through Jailkhani's equation of it with the national interest in certain circumstances and Chadwick's pragmatic approach, to Suter's reminder that the public interest may also be served outside those broadcasting organisations specifically established to serve it. We intend in this chapter to explore the extent of this field.

In the past half-century there has been an expansion of market-driven thinking and practice on a scale without precedent, responding to developments in communications technologies which have, in turn, often created the funding for further expansion. Countries throughout the world have witnessed armies of economists committed to attaching a price to practically everything. 'I measure, therefore I am' has become the watchword in hundreds of different situations. Unsurprisingly, since many of the technological advances which have been made have occurred in their own spheres, broadcasting and the growth of new media have been as profoundly influenced by these developments as any other branch of human activity.

Two more changes have been occurring at the same time. First, governments and sections of the public have moved a considerable way from an approach to such things as education, transport and provision for the Arts, which was grounded in the recognition of a public interest, to a point where the role of the state is, first, challenged and, then, diminished in favour of private interests. The second change has been the elevation of individual choice to a leading position in the calendar of human rights, with consequences, good and bad, over a wide area of activities. The public interest in broadcasting, the starting point for older institutions and still a mainstay for some, often struggles to assert itself in defiance of the market.

Against this troubled background, Andrew Graham, Master of Balliol College, Oxford University in the UK, commented on current attitudes towards the public interest:

> I think... the acceptance of the term public interest has declined.... it was never a term as much accepted in the States as here and to the extent that it was accepted, it has probably declined even further in America than here. And probably economists have been, as a group of people, some of those most responsible for the decline of the notion of the public interest. The whole of the so-called 'Public Choice' theory in the States basically took the view that you could not rely on civil servants or politicians to have higher interests than

their own. Everything was reducible to self-interest – and so politics becomes just another kind of market-place. Once you've made that kind of move, then at most the public interest is no more than the aggregation of individual interests... I absolutely don't accept that the only thing which motivates human beings is self-interest. It's a convenient assumption for economists and it's driven the whole thrust of economic policy and a great deal else for the last thirty or forty years. But just because it's mathematically helpful and can easily be turned into good models and because it can be used to explain certain aspects of the market, doesn't mean that it explains the whole of human behaviour. It doesn't. So, if you really want to have some notion of the public interest you have to step outside this narrow framework and recognise that human beings are more complex than economics assumes.

Andrew Graham's scepticism about the public interest in the US – where it was once described as nothing more than a device to preserve elite values[1] – was confirmed by Ed Baker, a Professor at the Annenberg School of Communications in Philadelphia, US:

> Those aren't terms used much among the circle I travel in. I would suspect that one might find people concerned with either trade or security talk about national interest – like bars on foreigners owning media entities might be justified in terms of national interest but these arguments don't really ring very loud.

However, there is one place in the US where the public interest is, or at least originally was, intended to exercise a weighty influence on the actions of a major federal agency. The Federal Radio Commission was created by the Radio Act, 1927, with five members – three from the ruling party, two from its rival – all appointed by the President. It represented an attempt to instil some discipline into the chaotic state of broadcasting in the Union, where the medium had become dominated by commercial interests. Companies were successfully defying attempts to strengthen the very limited licensing powers of the Department of Commerce. They were frequently at odds, arguing with one another over the use of frequencies and the relative strengths of their transmissions. In order to establish a criterion by which the Commission would judge the merits of future licence applications, the draftsmen adopted a phrase previously used in utilities legislation. Did the application, the Commissioners had to ask themselves, serve the 'Public interest, convenience and necessity?'[2] However, when they were considering proposals for new rail services, regulators were dealing with reasonably straightforward issues. By contrast, as the nature of broadcasting became more and more diverse, the meaning of 'the public interest' grew more difficult, subject increasingly to changes in technology, social needs and the pressures of competition. As a result, eight decades have been filled with debate about how the phrase is to be interpreted.

The phrase was to remain unchanged in 1934 when the new Communications Act replaced the word 'Radio' with 'Communications' in the Commission's title to become the Federal Communications Commission (FCC) and raised its membership to seven, although it was reduced again to five in 1983. 'Public interest, convenience or necessity' remains in place more than three quarters of a century later. The 1934 Act forbade the Commission from interfering with the exercise of free speech over the air, although an exception was made for obscenity, indecency and profane language. It was in almost all areas subject to hostile attacks by defenders of the First Amendment to the Constitution. The Amendment declares that 'Congress shall make no law.... prohibiting the freedom of speech, or of the press'. In courts ranging as high as the US Supreme Court, the Commission has won some fights over their interpretations of their duties and lost others. Historically, however, the 'public interest' criterion may be considered to have lost ground in the application of the principle and the rigour with which it has been pursued.

Monroe Price, also from the Annenberg School at the University of Pennsylvania, reflected whether, on the evidence of a recent case, the influence of the 'public interest' clause is set to wane further:

the question ... was whether the must carry rule which required the carriage of broadcast channels would cover the carriage of shopping channels. Ultimately the FCC said yes and it had to imply a theory that these were channels that were worthy of being licensed and being carried and it seemed to me that it was the kind of reductio ad absurdum of public interest – namely that in which the public was interested .... I think there's a shrinkage in the zone of decision making where public interest is relevant ... you could say the positive spin is that the shrinkage comes from the shift to multi-channel broadcasting.

A Washington DC Broadcast Attorney suggested that the shrinkage might have gone still further. Talking about the FCC and its regulation of format for radio licensees, she said,

> ...years ago [the FCC] specifically disallowed that they would ever look at radio stations' format... It is left to the market. In fact, some decades ago there was an appeal that the FCC decided that they did not want to be even thinking about format regulation and the court said, 'that was fine, you could leave it'. The current concept of the public interest, convenience and necessity could very well be the marketplace functioning on its own.

Ben Scott works for Free Press, a Washington-based non-profit-making organisation with a remit to promote public education in communications policy. It acts in the same area as a public interest advocate. He said,

> You cannot force the market to do that which it does not want to do and to attempt to try to force it to do that is either to engage in content regulation that is going to violate the First Amendment or to give content regulatory authority to federal regulators who will then become the arbiters of what is fair. What is in practice the reality is that the commercial broadcasters do everything they can to undermine the public interest obligations that are put upon them. If you look at the history of public service requirement you see a gradual erosion. You see litigation. You see regulatory proceedings to soften the requirement. You see exemptions. You see waivers. You see people violating them and taking the $5000 dollar fine as the cost of doing business.

However, the words are resolutely defended by Reed Hundt, who, appointed by President Clinton, served as Chair of the FCC between 1993 and 1997. Interviewed in Washington in the autumn of 2007, he challenged the definition of the public interest criterion given by one of his Republican predecessors, Mark Fowler.[3] Fowler had said that the public interest was what interested the public. Hundt's criticisms extended beyond Fowler to question some current economic orthodoxies:

> Mark's a friend of mine and I've always said to him directly what I would say to you which is that, you know that's just a word, you've turned an important idea into planned words and you've ridiculed it

in doing so and you know if what you mean is the same thing that Prime Minister Thatcher meant when she said, 'there's no such thing as society', then say that's what you mean. Well, what she meant in the full context, or as I understand it or interpreted it, was 'there's no such thing as society', and I believe the rest of her words were, 'there is only family and friends'. Meaning she didn't recognise that there was or that there are one's connections between relative strangers or that there's a fabric of community that stretches outside personal acquaintance networks. If you don't believe that, then you become indifferent to externalities and you become extremely, acutely, indifferent to public goods. Because there's no point in aspiring to create a public good unless you believe that there's such a thing as society. So if you're Mark Fowler and Maggie Thatcher who both were in office at the exact same time, different posts, different countries, you are saying something very similar when you say the public interest is only what the public is interested in.

In applying a test to the nature of the public interest in any potential decision to award a broadcasting licence, Hundt believed that it must fall within three parameters. The first was technology, meaning the manner of its delivery; the second economics, how it was to be funded; and the third the social landscape, the group, large or small, to which a service was to be directed. Together, they could be compared to the dimensions of a box, its height, length and width.

So you look at those three parameters and how they interact and that defines if you will, the situation in which you then say, 'okay what is the public interest?' ... Those are all ways of easily visualising some portion of society interest in some particular situation which might be to maximise economic welfare and be indifferent to the allocation of the gains. That might be the case. You might say, all we want is for there to be more wealth and we don't care in this particular case about how the wealth is allocated. If that's the thing, the public interest (will then) point you fairly directly to an almost pure economics approach to addressing the problem. But in some other case you might say, 'you know what we want to do here, because of maybe the social parameter, we want to make sure that we are creating a public good'. A good as to which any new user doesn't raise the total cost. A good, like a park, where you know if one more person drops by in Hyde Park, nobody gets charged anything for it or has to pay any more and it doesn't really have a meaningful impact on the upkeep, because it's paid for by whoever pays for Hyde Park grass cutting. So you might say that, that's what you want to do and in that case you won't look just to economics. You'll look to other disciplines to figure out how to create the public good. So the public interest is meant to be mutable but it always ought to be explained and it should never be that it is made the subject of a word game.

The public interest and the national interest

Because of the uncertainty about where one interest ends and the other begins, it may be useful to label some of the interests 'national' in a group which has been defined elsewhere as defensive. The most important of these is national defence, with public emergencies such as mass epidemics or energy shortages close behind – in short, those things which, threatening forcibly to disrupt or destroy the continuation of the national life or the unity of the nation, demand action from the government. There is another group ranking less immediately urgent, but with longer-term effects on the nation, such as the security of its food supplies, the continuing quality of its democracy and its internal administration, the maintenance of urban and rural industries, the preservation and further enrichment of its language and the education of its children not only academically but in the absorption of social values. After that there are cultural subjects ranging from the maintenance of traditional skills through the practice of the creative arts to the preservation of language. Unlike almost all the interests in the defensive group, almost every interest included in the second and third groups is capable of different interpretations, any one of which may be the most appropriate for a particular set of circumstances.

In recommending the formation of the British Broadcasting Corporation (BBC) in 1927, a British Government Committee described the future governing body as trustees of the national interest in broadcasting. In contemporary Britain, invocations of the national interest provoke the scepticism born of the over-reliance of politicians on the phrase to justify unworthy causes. However, in the late 1920s, only a decade away from the end of the First World War, the words used then may have resounded more profoundly for the generations which had survived the War.

In India, for example, where content regulation is in the hands of the government pending the long-delayed passage of a Broadcasting Bill, the two terms are often considered synonymous. Rakesh Kacker, formerly of the Telecommunications Regulatory Authority of India (TRAI), spoke first of India's national interest:

Public interest must include national interest but what people mean by national interest, for example, is that we should not have content from, say, Pakistan or wherever else...But the major concern (about) security and these kind of issues is from Pakistan. Because there are major concerns that Pakistan is very active in India, is propping up militant groups in India, is propping up terrorism in India. You don't find that with Bangladesh, or Sri Lanka or China....And I think Pakistan has similar concerns about India.

Then he described a different concern, domestic rather than national, but still in his view qualifying as a matter of national interest:

Society here is very conservative. Although you will find in the media criticism of excessive control of content, we can't get away from the fact that this is required. And wherever you find discussions with the political class, all of them have similar concerns about this kind of cultural degradation. Very often the point is made that you have similar content over the Internet. That is true. What you have over the Internet is far more than you have over television. But then Internet is confined to a smaller section of the population. Television, there is much wider reach. So certainly we do need regulation and the best way to do it is through an independent body outside the government.... I mean there is always a debate about where the line is drawn.... But rather than governments doing it directly, certainly the best way is an independent body doing it, (made up of) experts.

Prasar Bharati (the Broadcasting Corporation of India) has the responsibility of overseeing the country's public broadcasting, carried out in television by Doordarshan and in radio by All India Radio (AIR). Section 12 of the Bill establishing Prasar Bharati in 1990, after giving it the primary duty of informing, educating and entertaining the public, prescribes a number of specific obligations. These are set out in the Appendix. Baljit Singh Lalli, the Chief Executive Officer, expressed its purposes:

Basically the idea is that a public broadcaster has, would have to, take care of morality in our society, democratic values, secularism, and then to promote the cultural diversity at the same time, the oneness of society... And to ensure that there is some kind of healthy concourse between the policy-makers and implementers of the public policy and those for whom the policies are made, so we provide a forum through our programmes

The people, he said, must be made more aware of the institutions established to bring Indian democracy alive. Ashok Jailkhani, Deputy Director of Doordarshan, the public service television channel, expressed the commitment of the service to this idea:

We have social concerns. We have concerns for information, you know and we have a mandate for trying to be a catalyst for social change so all those duties are still with us as a public broadcaster.

Barry Melville, General Manager of the Community Broadcasting Association of Australia (CBAA), was asked if he thought there was a distinction between the national interest and the public interest in broadcasting: He answered,

I've been doing CBAA conferences for 15 years and never do I hear discourse about the national interest. We talk about the good solid work we do in representing diversity and upholding particular and diverse communities of interest, we make various value claims that this leads to national cohesion. This is a particularly strong argument in the ethnic broadcasting subsector of community broadcasting, that perhaps one of their strongest validity claims is that they keep people from a variety of ethnic community cultural backgrounds talking to each other and coexisting and responding to both their particular communities of interest but also coexisting as cooperating communities of interest on stations and upholding ethnic community broadcasting. So it is at that point I mostly hear the term the national interest in community cohesiveness. But I wouldn't say that the national interest itself bears very strongly in those kinds of considerations.

Although there is in Australian broadcasting a consistent emphasis on nation-building, whether it is cast as social cohesion or community awareness, the Deputy Chair of the Australian Communications and

Media Authority, Lyn Maddock, said the concept of the national interest was not often invoked:

> It's not a debate which has had any purchase in Australia in this area. In that context the debate has focussed on the 'public interest'. We've just been doing some work on how we might define the public interest because there is a whole range of ways of defining it in economics and we've been looking at that. And whether we go public with that or whether we use it privately to guide our actions we haven't yet decided. But this is where the debate in Australia has focussed.

Mark Armstrong, a former Chair of the ABC and now at Network Insight, a research institute in Melbourne, had no doubt of the national interest served by the creation of the SBS. The broadcaster had been founded to reflect the cultures and meet the needs of the many immigrants into Australia, something which, as an aspect of nation building, the ABC was considered to have neglected.[4] But Andrew Stewart, a lawyer in private practice dealing with media issues in Australia, while acknowledging that on occasion the two concepts could overlap, saw other occasions where the distinction was important:

> I think the government is there to represent the national interest, not the broadcasters. If you look at terrorism for example, there's a real tension between what might be in the national interest in suppressing information versus what's in the public interest about receiving information on the same topic. There you see the truly different nature of those two interests. It may be in the national interest (to suppress information) about someone accused of terrorist crime because the information may prejudice ongoing investigations, may prejudice proceedings in other jurisdictions. The public clearly have a very significant degree of interest in knowing about ongoing investigations into terrorist activities, on what basis police bring charges or choose not to bring charges and in believing that the judicial system copes well with those kinds of allegations.... Occasionally, you'll get times when the public interest has to give way or has to incorporate the national interest – give way is the better (term) – sometimes they will be coincident. It won't always be in the public interest for people to know everything about terrorist activities for example but they are two different things a lot of the time.

In Britain, the BBC's Director-General, Mark Thompson, thought that public and national interests existed side by side in what the Corporation's new Charter calls its Public Purposes.[5] There are six of them by which the BBC's performance is judged. They are in summary

> Sustaining citizenship and civil society; promoting education and learning; stimulating creativity and cultural excellence; representing the UK, its nations, regions and communities; bringing the UK to the world and the world to the UK; and, in pursuing its other purposes, helping to deliver to the public the benefit of emerging communications technologies and services, and taking a leading role in the switchover to digital television.

The last Public Purpose requires the BBC to help in the delivery of the benefits of emerging communications technologies to the public and taking a leading role in the switchover to digitalisation. Thompson commented,

> This is a part of the straightforwardly national policy around the future of broadcasting, around a significant part of the national infrastructure, national use of spectrum and so forth. I think the word 'national' and the digital switchover programme is a great thing and I think the word 'national' is the right word to use. It's politically led, and the public – or their representatives – have gone for it.

He believed that the term 'national interest' could also be applied to

> ...the relationship between the BBC World Service and the Foreign Office...the UK's own objectives about the British voice around the world. Again I can see something which I would call 'the national interest' there.

It seems that a national interest can be defined as one which concerns an objective set by government policy – the introduction of digitalisation in one case and the making of Britain's case around the world in the other. However, it is also clear that these objectives have to be ratified by public assent from outside Parliament – media, civil society and others – as well as inside.

For those who worked in the new media technologies industry, the term 'public interest' was not meaningful. It was felt to prescribe values that were not relevant in a highly interactive environment. The values that were offered by such services were content or programming material that was of value and interest for the individual user or community group.

Prescribing public service broadcasting

Although governments prescribe the nature of the programming to be produced by the broadcasters, whether predominantly or to a limited extent engaged in practising public service broadcasting, it is they who also create the initial situation in which the broadcasters have to operate. Universality of coverage has been one of the leading principles to be observed. No matter how remote the citizen is, he/she is entitled to services for which he/she, as a taxpayer, is paying.

Jock Given at the Swinburne Institute of Social Research at Melbourne University described the efforts of Australian governments to fulfil public service objectives, not least in the way special obligations have been placed on commercial broadcasters in return for concessions in taxation policies and the gifting of frequencies.

To pursue public interest objectives in Australia, we have [designated] National Broadcasters, as has been the case in many other countries. We have adopted a number, as other countries have, a number of different kinds of policy instruments, the case in many countries, and we have funded them. We have provided funding assistance to invest in the production of Australian dramas, documentary, children's programmes. We have imposed Australian content requirements requiring certain minimum levels of Australian programming to be transmitted on commercial networks and then programme specific quotas requiring minimum levels of high-end drama, locally produced drama, and documentary programmes as well. ...we have continued to invest money in new analogue transmission for areas that have received no terrestrial coverage before, while we were launching digital terrestrial services in major centres and talking about the importance of moving the whole television system to digital transmission: at the very same time we were investing money in getting analogue terrestrial television (to) communities in remote areas for the first time. So I think it's a sign of quite how important that has been politically: to get free to air broadcasting services as close to universally available as possible.

Asked about the justification for the imposition of special programming obligations on commercial and free-to-air services and whether they would continue, Bridget Fair at Seven Network, one of the three Australian free-to-air services, answered,

> Well, I guess it's a historical thing based on spectrum scarcity that we, like most other terrestrial broadcasters around the world, were in the privileged position of being given one of the very few available licences to provide these kind of services. As a result, we were also required to meet certain obligations and that [is the] equation, although the spectrum scarcity thing has arguably changed, although I don't think in reality, yet, certainly not in Australia where the government decided to issue only 3 commercial television licences for the foreseeable future in any event. People say the spectrum scarcity thing doesn't hold up anymore. I'm not sure that that's really the case. In any event, people's expectations of commercial television and free to air television in general are very high. 98 percent of people are able to receive services in Australia. There's an expectation you will get high quality free television services and people have always felt a certain degree of ownership over our services.... In addition to local origination and children's programmes...we have a requirement to contribute to adequate and comprehensive services under the Broadcasting Services Act. That means you don't all have to do every aspect of a comprehensive service but, together, there has to be a comprehensive service. Our Code of Practice has to be registered by the regulator after community consultation to ensure it meets community standards. So if there's a strong view that broadcasters ought to be doing one thing or another with their programming, then that will be reflected in the renewal processes for those Codes, which happen every three years.

The triennial reviews of the separate codes of practice which each sector of the industry must have are carried out by the ACMA.

Debra Richards, CEO of the Australian Satellite Television and Radio Association (ASTRA), believed that free-to-air commercial television has had its privileges extended, not entirely without cost, but leaving these broadcasters placed more advantageously than some of their competitors.

> There is still a view in Parliament that commercial television is the dominant player and therefore attracts more regulation. The

principle of the Broadcasting Services Act of 1992 is that the more influential you are, the more rules that you have associated with you. It doesn't seem to work for us, we have plenty of rules. But the thing is that they are still protected... there is still a protected oligopoly, so there is no fourth or fifth or sixth commercial network allowed. And my view is that until that is blown up to pieces; we won't really get true diversity in our industry. An aside: Their argument is that they need continued protection to deliver the so-called public service, community service obligations that they have... they only pay a percentage of their revenue for that spectrum. It's valuable public spectrum and, it's part of that, the quid pro quo for that, is that they deliver Australian content and children's television programmes and now, since they were gifted the digital space, they also have to caption or close-caption all primetime and all News and Current Affairs.

The imprecise nature of the public interest as it appears in the FCC's prescription was shared for a long time in the UK. Never formally set down, the role of the BBC Governors from the Corporation's foundation in 1927 was to protect the national interest which they were relied upon to be able to identify. They maintained their monopoly of both radio and television until 1954 when the Television Act created the Independent Television Authority (ITA), itself an interesting compromise between two views of the public interest within the Conservative Party. One group was made up from a new breed of more entrepreneurial members, claiming to be ten years younger on average than those who disagreed with them, among whom, at least initially, were Winston Churchill and most of his senior party colleagues.[6]

The Authority's 12 members represented a roll-call of what is known in the UK as the 'Great and Good', drawn from the same groups within society as the Governors of the BBC: senior figures from industry, commerce, education, Trades Unions and administration. No explicit commitment to securing the public interest was demanded of them.

In 2002, the government launched a new Communications Bill which, among other things, created a converged regulator, Ofcom, which absorbed five existing regulators.[7] As the Bill was making its way through Parliament, there were concerns among critics that the drift of the legislation was towards the values of the market, with an undue emphasis on the public as consumers rather than as citizens. After a considerable struggle in Parliament, the Bill's critics secured concessions from the government which made a clear distinction between consumer-interests and citizen-interests. The former included questions of reception and costs, the latter issues of content and the resolution of grievances about programmes. Nevertheless, the Bill remained heavily influenced by market-thinking, and Ofcom, once it had become operational, faced criticism for an undue concern over market-issues and a neglect of content.

Aware of growing pressure for a definition of public service which could be used to resist competition challenges from a market-driven European Union, the government inserted into the Bill a section describing the kinds of programming to be encompassed within the term 'public service broadcasting' as its expression of the public interest in broadcasting.[8] The Bill became law in 2003 as the Communications Act.

In June 2004 the BBC published, in *Building Public Value*, an account of its approach to an assessment of the value to the public of what it was doing or what it proposed to do.[9] In a prologue, Michael Grade, then Chairman of the BBC Trust, the body created to replace the Board of Governors at the start of the new Charter in 2006, expressed the BBC's purpose:

[The] BBC, placing the public interest before all else, will counterbalance that market-driven drift towards programme-making as a commodity.

The Trust has a duty to scrutinise every proposal from the BBC Executive to introduce new channels or amend the purposes of those already established. Each proposal must be scrutinised for its value to the individual, its citizen value and its economic value. Then, the document observes that – it is difficult to avoid the thought that one eye was directed towards Ofcom – citizen value and, to an extent, individual value call for delicate judgements. Measurement, it might have added, was not enough.

The broadcasting industry outside the BBC had had a long-standing grievance that the BBC, in a dominant position, was able to extend its activities with no real scrutiny of the effect they might have on the market. As a result, a market impact assessment was included in the process by which the BBC Trust reviewed such proposals. Ofcom carries out the assessment, overseen by a Joint Steering Committee formed between Ofcom and the Trust. This process has to be completed within three months of its initiation. The Trust has the final word, but its freedom, in the view of Steven Barnett of the University of Westminster, is severely constrained, first by the tests which the Trust must itself apply, but also by its obligation to consider the interests of industry which enjoys powerful Press support.[10]

The six Public Purposes, already summarised, play a major role in the overall process of assessment. Georgina Born of Cambridge University in the UK, a sceptic about the purposes of Ofcom and about the BBC's importation of Ofcom's performance measurement framework into its *Building Public Value* document (BPV), nonetheless considered that the text had found a way to mitigate the negative impact of that framework:

I was critical at the time because [BPV] represented a blatant capitulation to introducing performance measures into the BBC and the whole language represented by Ofcom... So I thought 'Oh, my God, if the BBC goes this route, how can you ever defend values, such as quality, risk or innovation, and related activities that are intrinsically non-quantifiable?' On the other hand, if you look at that document [BPV], it is actually rather clever because there are sections of it where they pick up questions like 'Well, it's tricky to transform qualitative judgements into quantitative measures. Sometimes this will be difficult'. There are lists and then there are these attempts to fill out how one might be able to do this. And they list various kinds of qualitative criteria... you know, innovation, diversity, all those kinds of issues and they develop them and do sub-headings – it's a very clever attempt... I was really impressed to see the thinking which was going into somehow making this nebulous set of round values fit into these square performance measurement holes. And I guess it convinced me that it wasn't impossible, that you could do something like this. And if you also stressed the fact that at the same time qualitative judgements at the margins have to be made, you could somehow make these things work and make the qualitative issues meet the measurement indicators.

The BBC Charter, risking some confusion, refers to both licence-fee payers and the public. An explanation was provided by Penny Young, Head of Audiences at the BBC Trust:

We certainly don't mean 'licence fee payer' only to mean the person who actually pays for the licence. We mean everyone. We do still tend to talk about 'licence-fee payers' as a way of trying to distinguish from the 'audience'. This is a false distinction in many ways – but it shows that we're listening to people at a slightly more strategic level, and in their role as people who publicly fund the BBC.

She went on to consider the difference between consumers and citizens:

> We will always be particularly interested in what people value for themselves. If the BBC doesn't provide something of real value for the majority of the public – something they personally value and love – then the future of the BBC as a publicly funded organisation must be at risk. That's the consumer bit. But clearly the citizen aspect is important as well – particularly where the public values content being provided whether they personally consume it or not, and particularly where content is at risk of not being provided anywhere else. The public buy into this argument too – and recognise, for example, that children's programming is vital, whether or not their own family consume it.

Nicholas Kroll, Director of the BBC Trust, was asked where, under the Charter, the primacy lay between the interests of the licence-payers, broadly defined, and those of industry. Echoing Reed Hundt's image of a box, he said that it was necessary to proceed

> issue by issue, case by case . . . I can imagine a BBC proposition . . . as being of moderate detriment to some broadcasting interests and absolutely enormous difficulty to others, You're going to have reach a judgement as to what's the field against which you're judging this proposition.

Later in the interview, he said that he did not believe that

> licence-payers were served simply by having a BBC. There are interests in the licence-fee payers having a plural broadcasting marketplace.

This view was developed by Andrew Ramsay of the Department for Culture, Media and Sport (DCMS), the department responsible for broadcasting in the UK:

> I think the licence-fee payers have primacy, but it doesn't mean to say that dealing with the interests of other broadcasters and the rest of the industry isn't very important. But I think if you look at the position of the licence-fee payers as we did, you'll see what we mean . . . . It's not just about what appears on the BBC, (the Trust has) to be conscious about what licence-fee payers in the rest of their life are

getting and if the BBC acted in such a way that they destroyed competition and there was no plurality etc. etc. that wouldn't necessarily be in the benefit of licence-fee payers. It's actually in the interests of licence-fee payers that the rest of the market functions and the BBC doesn't prevent that happening.

In Australia, the two public service broadcasters, ABC and SBS, designated as National Broadcasters, operate under Charters which are included in their governing statutes enacted respectively in 1983 and 1991. The ABC's services are directed to its domestic audiences and its obligations to represent Australia and its attitudes to world affairs to the wider world. In the SBS Act, the broadcaster is required to provide multilingual and multicultural services that inform and entertain all Australians and, in doing so, to reflect Australia's multicultural society. Both Acts include more detailed specifications for the respective outputs of the two organisations. The two Charters are reproduced in the Appendices.

The US Corporation for Public Broadcasting (CPB) was founded in 1967 when President Johnson took up a proposal by the Carnegie Foundation for the establishment of such a Corporation. Congress declared that it was in the public interest to encourage the growth and development of public radio and television, including the use of such media for instructional, educational and cultural purposes. At that time, mired in Vietnam, the President may have been hoping that a publicly funded service would give the government more support. As Erik Barnouw comments, the early moves were not very encouraging from a liberal perspective. Johnson set the first year's budget at a lowly four-and-half million dollars and his first appointee as Chair, a former Secretary of the Army, commissioned as his first research project a study on riot control.[11] However, in 1969, the CPB created the Public Broadcasting Service (PBS) and, in 1970, National Public Radio as the means by which federal funds could be channelled to individual stations across the US. The Department of Education supported the educational programme, *Sesame Street*, which would become a success on a global scale.

Funding the broadcasters

In India, Doordarshan and AIR, regulated by Prasar Bharati, receive grants from the government and take advertising and sponsorship. In Australia, ABC receives government grants while SBS, the second

National Broadcaster, receives grants and revenues from advertising and sponsorship. Controversially, it also receives revenue from product placement (the practice of displaying commercial products prominently in programmes). Although not formally designated as public service broadcasters, other organisations in Australia, commercially funded, are gifted spectrum in return for producing prescribed kinds of output, judged by the regulator to fall within the public interest, for example, programmes for children and locally originated material. Local production is a requirement imposed on Australian subscription television, but, although it has to be paid for, there is no compulsion to produce or transmit.

There are three public service broadcasters in the UK: the BBC, Channel 4 and S4C, the Welsh-language service. They differ in the arrangements made for their funding. The BBC is mainly financed by a receiving licence-fee payable by households, although it is now drawing a considerable amount of additional funding from BBC Worldwide, which operates partially on a commercial basis. Channel 4 was established as a non-profit-making company dependent upon advertising revenue and competing with fully commercial services as well as the BBC. The Welsh channel is funded by a government grant and advertising. In addition, ITV[12] and Five, which operate national commercial services, have residual PSB obligations for News and Current Affairs, the only form of output now mandated by Ofcom.

The circumstances in which, through the creation of the CPB, the notion of state intervention in the funding of broadcast services was introduced into American broadcasting were discussed earlier.[13] In addition to the Corporation's funding of the stations through the PBS and National Public Radio, stations also draw revenue from individual states, advertising, sponsorship and donors, making public appeals for financial support a regular feature of their programming, discussed earlier in this chapter. Major projects may receive grants from the US National Fund for The Endowment of the Arts.[14] The CPB's mission statement acknowledges a commitment to invest the funds provided by Congress in programmes that are educational, innovative, locally relevant and reflective of America's common values and cultural diversity. It is a commitment which would find its place comfortably alongside those of public service broadcasters elsewhere. It also suggests that the existence of common values should be added to Reed Hundt's placing of society at the heart of the public interest.

Broadcasting and beyond: Preserving the public interest

Advancing further into the twenty-first century, the public interest in broadcasting is confronted by three dilemmas. The first of them is concerned with funding: the willingness of the public to provide the necessary financial support, either directly or through governments and Parliaments, to fulfil everything which the public interest might be thought to demand. The second relates to the means by which, in broadcasting and the new media, the public interest can be served. The fragmentation of the mass audiences generated in the heydays of the major networks, publicly funded or commercial, has raised the question of the scale on which those networks should continue. Is there something irreplaceable in their critical mass, sustaining quality and diversity and thereby serving that national interest described in the section above? Or should these networks, to whatever extent, change in character to reflect the public dialogue which has been stimulated by the Internet, the amount of networking by individuals which it has generated and the rise of the blog with its implications for the democratic process? The great majority of under-20-year-olds in Australia, the UK and the US, as well as a growing number of them in India, have not known a world without the Internet with all the ease and fluidity of the conversations it stimulates. Should we be looking forward to the day when the nature and extent of the public interest would be the subject of online debate culminating in a vote? And if we do, do we experience hope or misgivings?

Three different perspectives on how the future might develop are offered, one from Britain and two from Australia. The first is from Mark Armstrong, Australia:

For 5 years I was the Chair of the ABC Board, but long before that I was a passionate supporter of public broadcasting. In our country, I've found it very disappointing that a lot of people who think they're champions of public broadcasting want to support a single channel comprehensive service, or even a single package of channels, where so much of the money is spent on almost duplicating sport or general entertainment programmes or programmes that are bought from overseas of exactly the same kind as commercial TV buys. Why should the very scarce resource of the public funding for public broadcasters be spent on things that will be broadcast anyway? What citizen cares which channel they receive the material on – the important point is that it's there. Now there's another argument about keeping the integrity of a public broadcaster for example with drama, to keep enough drama to be produced by a public broadcaster to ensure they've got the skills, they've got the esprit de corps, they've got the critical mass, but that's quite different from saying the public broadcasters should waste their budget on things the public might see anyway.

Robin Foster – former Partner of Ofcom, UK, and now an independent adviser – from whom the following quotation comes, spoke about one of the problems now confronting the public and the policy makers as they look at the future.

The argument would be that as audiences fragment, it becomes harder to put together the finance to pay for high-quality, high-production value programming. Now the counter-argument to that, which I have heard made, is that, well, yes, but producers will be able to find finance and also the new media gives programme makers the opportunity to use and re-use and re-release the programmes over time and tap into other sources of revenues. I think that the suggestion is that financing television programmes becomes much more like financing of films where you have to put together funding for a whole range of different distribution outlets rather than relying on one lump sum up front from the BBC or ITV. In theory that sounds fine to me. I think in practice it means that certain types of programmes probably will find it harder to go down that route than others. It will be much easier to raise the money for high-profile talent, for tried and tested successes and that sort of thing, so you may find that the more innovative, more off-the-wall, less obvious programming finds it harder to get funding. And I think there is a big question-mark for public interest intervention in future. That may be where we have to think hardest about finding the public funds to continue to support that sort of programming. That's where I think the future evolution of today's public broadcasters will still be important. I think you still need ways of funding innovative content and then helping audiences find out about new programming and new talent. So the challenge is going to be for the main broadcasters of the future to still have a key-role in packaging. A promotional role, helping you select things that you are going to enjoy. The worry, I suppose, for the packagers, if that is what you call them for a moment, is that there are all sorts of other ways of doing that now. You only have to go onto the Internet to see how there is huge emphasis or value placed on other users' recommendations. So you can go to YouTube and see what the top videos of the day are. You don't necessarily have to rely on a tried and trusted organisation or brands to do it for you. Nevertheless, I still firmly believe that those tried and trusted brands will have an important role to play in aggregating content and aggregating viewers together. They probably won't look like linear channels. They might look more like Internet portals in the future, but they still will be there helping you choose what to watch and suggesting things that you might enjoy.

The third quotation is from Bruce Meagher, Director of Strategy and Communications for SBS. He was asked how the public broadcaster defined itself when there were so many creators reflecting Australian culture, producing material which had traditionally been the broadcasters' preserve.

First, the potential to do something of a higher standard than you certainly can produce through those smaller user-generated things, and the second thing is a quality control, Quality is certainly a vexed term, but if you come to the public broadcaster, there are going to be certain standards applied in terms of ethical standards of journalism, balance and all those other obligations that we have to adhere to. That we will seek to portray a wide range of opinions and not just in the News and Current Affairs, that you'll find perspectives and viewpoints that you won't find in other places. I suppose, that in a fragmenting world, where can you go to be sure of some level of quality control and certainty? It's not just public broadcasters, but quality brands should be able to offer people a place to go where they know that certain standards apply and that a particular editorial judgement is being made or whatever the criteria is. To the extent that there is selection going on of material that it's done within a particular framework that helps the consumer navigate an otherwise very difficult world. And I think that, if public broadcasters want to succeed in that realm it has to be very largely driven by original content. Because increasingly you'll be able to go around aggregators of content. If you're just someone who pulls together Warner Bros well, why won't Warner Bros sell direct, and it's already happening that people go and download the whole season of *Lost* or whatever before it comes anywhere near Australian television. It is interesting to see people grappling with that.

One sceptical interviewee compared state intervention with a charging rhinoceros – difficult to stop once started.

For most members of an older generation in the four countries under study, the major broadcasting organisations have been dominant features in their lives. In India, although television has reached only a limited section of the rural population, often through communal receivers, radio has spread more widely. For all, the future holds the prospect of institutional changes certain to transform a familiar landscape. At the core of preserving the public interest in broadcasting lies the question of the degree to which continuation of intervention by the state, in the form of revenue-raising through the licence-system or grants-in-aid, makes good what might once have been called 'market-failure', but may now more appropriately take the name of 'market shortfall', favoured by Robin Foster:

> ...the mainstream thinking on public service broadcasting over the years...broadly said there were a lot of quite wide-ranging objectives which should be provided by different types of public intervention in the UK...(tending) to take the view that certain things were desirable whatever the market was going to deliver and in fact it was desirable for some of them to be delivered outside of the market for various reasons. And I contrasted that approach with the economics-based market failures approach, which took the market as a starting point and then identified areas in which the market might not work very well, and that tended to lead towards a much narrower definition of public interest content. In thinking about those two approaches, it is possible that depending on the view taken of the market and depending on the view taken of social objectives, they might not be that different from each other in where they end up. However, they do tend to lead to either broader or narrower views of what public interest should be...My own belief at the moment is that the market failures approach is probably too narrow, but we can't ignore what the market provides...I've started to talk about market shortfalls which is intended to reflect the gap between what the market might provide and what we as a society might want to see. And that isn't necessarily just about a market failure; it may be about wider public policy provision. But the point I'm trying to make is that we should be clear about what the public policy objectives are, and shouldn't assume that they encompass everything that has been done in the past.

In considering the public policy objectives of which Foster was talking, it is important to maintain a distinction between the institutions which have hitherto been expected to deliver them and the objectives themselves if our societies are to take full advantage of the possibilities now opening up.

In Britain, for some years there has been a question as to whether PSB can exist in isolation from the institutions currently providing it. News Corporation's Sky Channel in Britain, resisting the status of a public service broadcaster with the obligations it brings, produces a well-respected, impartial and accurate news service, the winner of many professional awards. A claim for Sky News as a piece of PSB would be incontestable, but most unlikely to be made. Martin Le Jeune, who had been Head of Public Affairs at BSkyB, made this clear:

'Sky News' is deliberately not like that [BBC News]... It's not cavalier with its facts, but it aims to be faster than the BBC. But Sky is always very wary of anything that implies that it is doing it out of a sense of obligation on behalf of the PSB system. It is a channel which sets great store by its independence which is an essential part of its brand.

Andrew Kenyon of the Centre for Media and Communications Law in Australia commented,

You can say that historically you had a quid pro quo approach which included local content because it would be 'good for the nation', it would help the local industry, the politicians could get away with it, they thought it would be popular, for whatever reasons, and now, that doesn't look sustainable in the same way and you're going to have this incredibly diverse range of media sources. But there isn't a lot of evidence that the mass audiences will become so diverse. Most people still use... maybe this will change over time, there's a lag and it's not clear how long the lag will be, most people still use major commercial and public media sites.

In 1986, the Conservative Government in the UK set up a committee under Professor (now Sir) Alan Peacock to examine the financing of the BBC.[15] It was said that the government's expectation was that the Committee would recommend that the BBC should carry advertising and do away with the mystique which had attached itself over the years to the licence-fee. But the Committee found that if a move of that kind took place, the attraction of the BBC services to advertisers would inflict damage on the existing commercial television services by diverting advertising away from them. Instead, the Committee recommended that the link between the BBC, as its sole beneficiary, and the licence-fee should be ended. In future, the BBC should receive the proceeds of a diminishing licence-fee and a fund created to be competed for by the BBC and other broadcasters, the content of whose programmes were considered to qualify as public service, the Committee suggested.

Public service broadcasting has generally been thought of as applying as much to a philosophy of broadcasting as to individual programmes and therefore to entire schedules of programmes built upon the guiding principle of independence from political or commercial pressures. The idea of grafting public service programmes onto schedules built on commercial principles for commercial purposes seemed to be unrealistic from the outset. Audiences tended to be much more static in the past, but in the 20 years since Peacock reported in the UK, outlets of many different kinds have been developed, creating new viewing habits among the public. While devotion to linear channels remains strong, the appeal is growing of the more varied diet provided by the different products of digitalisation, the Internet, TIVO, iPods and television or video on demand. Under the influence of technology, public service television can itself be thought of as a series of individual projects. Mark Thompson, the BBC's Director-General, believes that 'public service content' would be a more appropriate description. For him, broadcasting will remain, but as a subset of public service content.

> ... what matters most is the body of content and what matters rather less than it used to is precisely how you access that content... What I would straightforwardly agree with is that the BBC News Website is public service. It's not broadcasting, it's literally not broadcasting, it's on the Web and it's public service content. And in a converging world it probably makes more sense to talk about 'public service content' rather than 'public service broadcasting'. Broadcasting will be – for decades – a very significant subset of public service content, but it will only be a subset. It already is, today, only a subset. I don't think that there is any reason to believe that intervention to create public service content will be any less necessary because of convergence. I do not believe that the transition from public service broadcasting to public service content, broadcasting plus Web plus interactivity and all the rest of it, means that the need for intervention is going to reduce. Nor do I think it is obvious that because it's content and not broadcasting, you don't need clear frameworks, structures, institutions and clear funding money.

Tim Suter of Ofcom offered a rather different picture of the future:

> I think once you move beyond broadcasting you get into a very much more interesting and diverse state and the sorts of ways in which you have allocated money for public broadcasting probably no longer work. If you think about where public money is spent online in creating communities and supporting communities, a huge amount of public money is already being spent. So there is not actually, as it were, a deficit in terms of public spending both online and in new forms of engagement, so the question is what are the new forms of content that you would want to have brought about, where should you be putting this money? Where is the market gap? Where is the market deficit that you'd be wanting this money to address? I think it's a rather different kind of institution, a rather different kind of model, than the one we have for public service broadcasting. I don't think we can expect the models of public service broadcasting to particularly translate...

In the years since the Peacock Report was published there has been much debate about its implications. The proposal for a central fund to which broadcasters might apply for support for their public service initiatives led to suggestions that there could be a public service publisher making and offering public interest material for use by both traditional broadcasters and new media.[16] The possibility of drawing on licence-fee revenue as the source of funding for activities outside the BBC, a practice known as top-slicing, has been raised by government ministers. The decision in 2007 to impose on licence-income the cost of funding digitalisation across the country prompted suggestions that rather than restoring these sums, pejoratively described as 'excess licence revenue', to the financing of the BBC's broadcasting services on completion of digitalisation, they should be diverted to other broadcasting activities. In the eyes of the BBC's supporters, the precedent set in the case of digitalisation is a dangerous one, further threatening the BBC's ability to maintain the comprehensive range of programmes and threatening the link, traditionally understood to be valued by a broad section of popular opinion, between the licence-payers and the BBC.

Tim Suter outlined some of the questions to be faced in the future:

> At the moment non-BBC public service broadcasting is funded by an individual subsidy: essentially it's cash revenue foregone by the Treasury through spectrum allocation and as spectrum scarcity unwinds

that implicit subsidy unwinds with it, so the question is what is the value of the subsidy now, because it clearly has a financial value, and if you were to take that sum of money, or indeed any sum of money, and say how could we spend it in future, how could we replace the implicit subsidy of the moment with an explicit subsidy in future: first of all, how would you do it; secondly, where would you spend it? Would you spend it on television, effectively subsidising those parts of television which commercial broadcasters would no longer find it sensible to make, like regional news or programmes for children? Or would you spend that money in different places to ensure a provision of public service content in what is still called new media for distribution in the future, the debates that we started last time around? The broad consensus seems to be that you should not spend the money really on television, you should spend the money in a new media environment. Spending it on television involves answering the question of how you could ensure that it is quite genuinely not going to support things that they would have made anyway.

News, democracy and the public interest

In the future foreseen by Tim Suter for British broadcasting, PSB in the sense it is now generally understood could be increasingly augmented by 'public service content', the phrase Mark Thompson used to describe services delivered through various platforms, like websites, which would not be classed as broadcasting.[17] Other possibilities already exist and more can be expected to develop in the next few years. Several of the interviewees for this book drew attention less to an overall shortage of funding than to the difficulties of countering market pressure which, observing Mark Fowler's dictum, would ensure that the public interest was interpreted as nothing more than that which interests the public. Nowhere, perhaps, is that pressure a greater threat than it is to the maintenance of an informed democracy, particularly through News and Current Affairs, but also elsewhere in the schedules and online. With a proliferation of outlets comes competition for markets. The variety of newspapers found in each of the four countries under review demonstrates that clear branding, from raucous tabloid to weighty broadsheet, is essential to commercial success, as it would be in the electronic media. Both style and content are of great importance to that success, but it can be won at the expense of several aspects of the public interest. Privacy provides a clear example of where a strong public interest exists, regularly conflicted between the public's right to know and the individual's right to have protection for certain details of his or her life. A second aspect is accuracy in the reporting of the facts upon which an audience can base its judgements, though, depending on how the evidence is construed by individuals or groups, the conclusions they draw may differ, just as their starting points differ in beliefs or experience. A third example is impartiality in the assembling and presentation of those facts and the cases that may be built upon them.

At the heart of the matter, however, is the establishment and retention of trust. No amount of safeguarding the qualities described above can protect them against an absence of trust among the public. Decline in trust has been a marked characteristic of the past half-century in many democratic societies. Scepticism about the actions and words of those in authority is a proper corollary of a belief in democracy, but that corollary is often translated into near-immediate and cynical disbelief. The general loss of trust has been linked, in Britain at least, to a falling-off in turnouts at elections and a disregard bordering on contempt for politicians, particularly, but by no means only, among younger people and some minority ethnic groups. The consequent threat to democracy is very real.

In the summer of 2007, the BBC was faced with a series of accusations of fake competitions, phone-ins and misleading editing. Accusations of a similar kind were made against ITV and Channel 4, resulting in a significant loss of trust in the three public service channels that were considered to have treated their audiences with contempt.[18]

The offence was unfair dealing and deception, the only consolation being derived from the episodes was that no malpractice had been reported from the News and Current Affairs outputs, where any compromise with accuracy or impartiality would have been disastrous.

The ABC, with a statutory obligation to impartiality in News and Current Affairs, also requires impartiality under its Editorial Policy Guidelines, which are applied in three distinct settings:

(i) Case by case to complaints about specific programmecontent and individuals.
(ii) More broadly across genres, networks, and platforms over time, and
(iii) Under statute to news and information.

In the early part of 2008, the ABC put into wide circulation a consultation paper on the theme of impartiality, recognising the rapid rate of changes affecting broadcasting and telecommunications.[19] The paper acknowledged that, in situations involving impartiality, a number of elements come into play according to the circumstances. They range from accuracy and even-handedness through context to the absence of prejudice in the making of editorial judgements at different levels of authority. The consultation process is continuing.

Under the Communications Act, 2003, the BBC, in common with other broadcasters, is bound to observe due impartiality in the treatment of matters of political or industrial controversy and matters of public policy.[20] The word 'due' is interpreted in the Ofcom Broadcasting Code as meaning adequate or appropriate to the subject of the programme. Factors to be considered in reaching a judgement, apart from the nature of the subject, include the type of programme and channel, the audience's expectation of the likely content of the programme, and the extent to which an indication of its content has been given to the audience. Due balance is equally required in a single programme or over a series.[21] The time of transmission would once have been another factor for consideration, but there is now less and less certainty when a programme will be viewed or listened to, so timing has lost much of its significance.

The BBC has recognised that, in securing public trust, the whole of its output must be involved. In 2007, at the time of the premium telephone rates scandal mentioned above, the BBC Trust set up a study of impartiality, accompanied by much research into public attitudes. The study, in setting out 12 principles, noted that the BBC was generally seen as impartial by the audience, and impartiality was both demanded and valued. With British society changing, impartiality, the study suggested, could no longer necessarily be represented in a simple division between opposing views. The provenance of those views was an element which increasingly had to be taken into account.

In the US, the National Association of Broadcasters (NAB) launched a code of practice in 1939 which, taking the scarcity of channels into account, said that news broadcasters should not editorialise and that the elucidation of news should be without bias. The Communications Act of 1937 provided that stations which allowed a candidate for political office to broadcast should give equal opportunities to rival candidates. The FCC, three years later, in a statement known as the Mayflower Doctrine, declared that broadcasters could not be advocates, but subsequently modified the ruling if contrary views were also aired. The ruling applied not simply to political opponents, but in general. What had become known as the Fairness Doctrine was upheld by the US Supreme Court in 1969 when the Commission faced a challenge from a station which had refused the right of reply to a personal attack.[22] When Congress proposed to turn the FCC's ruling into law in 1987, widening the scope of the 1937 Act, President Reagan, hostile in principle to regulation, vetoed the Bill. The Fairness Doctrine went into a slow decline, the case for it weakened as the political climate changed and the force of the scarcity arguments dwindled. In 1985, the FCC conceded that the Doctrine might have a chilling effect and even be in breach of the First Amendment. Two years later, the Doctrine with its particular interpretation of the Commission's public interest role was abandoned. The Democrats have suggested that it should be revived, but they have not survived Republican resistance.

In India, the Act establishing the regulator of public broadcasting, the Prasar Bharati Act, contains a provision in Section 2(b) which lays down as one of its duties that it should safeguard

> the citizen's right to be informed freely, truthfully, and objectively on all matters of public interest, national or international, and presenting a fair and balanced flow of information including contrasting views without advocating any opinion or ideology of its own.

What is the future for impartiality? It is closely, but not exclusively, connected with the issue of public funding. In Britain, the BBC's prolonged resistance to the argument that the licence-fee was a tax has been ended by a Treasury declaration that it is. So if public money from one form of taxation or another is being spent on a news service, it carries an obligation to observe impartiality in the service it provides for those who fund it.

Michael Grade, Executive Chairman of ITV – who is doubtful whether, with the ending of spectrum scarcity, any form of content regulation can continue for much longer – believes that commitments to impartiality and accuracy will both be casualties. While accuracy, he suggests, can be taken care of in the courts, he makes an exception to his conclusion that, with three billion pounds of public money going into the BBC, there can be no justification in the future for public intervention in the private sector. He argues, however, that it is not in the BBC's interests to be the only major supplier of impartial world, national and regional news.

Those who agree that current statutory restrictions on News and Current Affairs programmes in the UK have no more place in broadcasting than they would have in newspapers can point to the US, where television and radio are free to say very much what they like on controversial issues. Whether the quality of the democratic debate is improved as a result must be a matter of speculation by anyone outside the US. But the proposition that the public interest should be acknowledged in the practice of due impartiality by at least one, and preferably two, national channels should be an essential element in that debate. Even if within the private sector there is an operator who sees advantages in providing such a channel while accepting some constraints, currently the case with Sky Television in Britain, it would be wrong to place sole responsibility for the nation's news services in the hands of an organisation with duties to its investors. There is a real public interest in retaining impartiality into the future as the defining mark of at least one publicly funded channel. There is evidence from Britain, Australia and the US to suggest that this preference continues to be relatively firm and remains set to be so for some years to come, however varied the reasons for its persistence: habit, the popularity of programmes, resistance to new technology (rapidly diminishing) and a unifying element within families may play some part in households' decision-making.

Blogging has become another factor to be considered. The public is increasingly submitting news items in both words and pictures to the broadcasters and a proportion is being used on air, described as User Generated Content (UGC). The news is no longer an area exclusively for professional journalists. Images shown of the arrest of two of the 21st July terrorists in London in 2005 came from a member of the public. The BBC's Report on Impartiality refers to 12,000 pieces of UGC contributed on a single day of heavy snowfalls. The phrase 'citizen-journalists' is becoming a commonplace and has led to criticism in the US of a tendency in the Press to over-quote them as a collective expression of popular opinion. Attempts have been made there to develop codes of conduct for those still-exceptional bloggers who take their responsibilities as citizens no less seriously than they do their rights as journalists.[23] Bill Buzenberg of the Center for Public Integrity in Washington acknowledged the virtues of bloggers as well as recognising their limitations:

> They're part of a really interesting echo chamber going on and no one is going to stop them. The problem is that most of the blogosphere does not involve original reporting. A lot of it is citing content that was produced by a relatively few credible content producers. When the Center does a report we get tremendous blog traffic, meaning thousands of citations linking to the Center's latest report. I think this serves a wonderful purpose and does reach a large audience. But there are many other less credible sources than the Center for

Public Integrity; we are factual, solid, and you know you can count on the Center to get it right. We've done our own reporting and our own database and our own fact checking. It's not just a lot of opinion. That's certainly not true with a lot of what goes on in the blogosphere. Blogs can be nefarious too; they can bring down a Dan Rather[24] fairly or unfairly. So there is danger of misuse, too. It will be interesting to watch during the election campaign to see how the blogosphere can be misused by people with specific interests, generating charges, for example, that may or may not be true.

Sir Mark Tully, formerly the BBC's Correspondent in India, asked whether the new media would serve the public interest, was cautiously hopeful, replying that

In some ways, yes. They could do. Because neither are they dependent on commercial pressures nor are they dependent on the government. And it's going to be very difficult for the government to control the new media so insofar as the new media can lead to the flowering of lots of tiny little independent pathways and blogs, yes it could serve the public better. But my own feeling is that the new media have a huge problem and that is authenticity or reliability or credibility. How do you choose which blog to read? It may be that Joe Blogg, that you know happens to be a very good journalist, has a blog then you would think to yourself 'well, I'll read Joe Blogg's blog'. But supposing you don't know that, supposing it doesn't have ... How do you know about the authenticity of it, how do you know it doesn't have balance, bias? There is someone I met the other day for instance in Bangalore who is running a blog type thing and he said he is getting a wonderful reaction to it and he has broken two or three stories not broken by the national press, so, in theory, I think, yes, it could do (promote public interest) but how it's going to work out, it's quite early days yet.

Sagarika Ghose of CNN-IBN, a private news channel in India, spoke enthusiastically as a news broadcaster about the role of bloggers in her country:

The thing is the blogosphere in India is very lively. There are lots of people who are blogging ... There are lots of campaigns that bloggers do in India. For example, citizen's campaigns, activist campaigns, criminal justice campaigns, they're all on the net. And it's particularly relevant for India because of the huge diaspora, because of the huge numbers of people who are Indians working in the US, etc. They have a huge alumni happening. They use the Internet very effectively. I was very surprised the other day when I got a huge number of mails in my email saying 'Why have you written about the death of some-body in the Indian Army (who has been killed fighting the Kashmir militants)' and the media hadn't picked up the story and they were writing from Canada and America saying 'Why haven't you picked up this issue, why haven't you?' They provide a very important input.

She went on to talk about her own role as a journalist and a blogger:

There are lots of functions that a blog fulfils in a country like India. My reasons for writing a blog...I have to write an article but I post it up as a blog because I am interested in being provocative, and I'm interested in seeing where people stand on issues. You know lots of issues in India are being worked out. We are still confused about caste, about religion, about gender and as a broadcaster, someone who is trying to reach out to people and trying to get people to think about issues or communicate the dilemmas of people to a wider public, I want to know what people are thinking. I want to know what they are reacting to, what the issues are. That's why I write my blog.

In the new circumstances created by new media forms such as blogging, the broadcaster cannot apply many of the tests for impartiality which he/she would to material generated in-house and which were discussed earlier in this chapter. Faced with the torrent of individual opinions and information which flows every day, the public good requires within it institutional frameworks enjoying public trust and capable of mediation as well as of answering the question 'To the sound of whose axe are we listening?'

Notes

1. Krattenmaker, T. & Powe, L.A. *Regulating Broadcast Programming*, Cambridge, Mass., MIT Press, 1994.
2. Section 4 of the Act states that the Commissioners '*from time to time, as public interest, convenience or necessity requires, shall...*' followed by a prescription of their duties.
3. Mark Fowler a Reagan-era appointment, was in office as Chair of the FCC between 1981 and 1987.
4. See also Chapter 4, Australia.

5. BBC Charter, Article 4.
6. Wilson H.H. *Pressure Group passim*, Secker & Warburg, London, 1961.
7. The Independent Television Commission (regulator of commercial television), the Radio Authority (overseer of commercial radio), the Office of Telecommunications, the Broadcasting Standards Commission and the Radiocommunications Agency.
8. Section 464(A) of the Act is attached as Appendix iv.
9. BBC, *Building Public Value*, 2004.
10. Barnett, S. *Can the Public Service Broadcaster Survive? Renewal and Compromise in the New BBC Charter in* Lowe, GF and Bardoel, J. *Public Service Broadcasting to Public Service Media*. RIPE@2007 Nordicom, 2008.
11. Barnouw, E. *A History of Broadcasting in the United States*, Vol. iii., Oxford University Press, New York, 1970, pp. 293–95.
12. The company has given notice that it will wind down its output of children's programmes which, under Ofcom's predecessor, had been mandated.
13. P. 61 above.
14. Support for the highly successful children's series *Sesame Street* came from the US Department of Education.
15. *Committee on the Financing of the BBC*. Cmnd 9284. London. HMSO 1986.
16. In a speech to the Royal Television Society on 11 March, 2008, Ed. Richards, Chief Executive of Ofcom, appeared to suggest that the concept of a Public Service Publisher, promoted by Ofcom for several months, had been intended only to encourage the view that public service content could be accommodated among new media as well as in mainstream channels. This particular concept appears now to have been taken off the board, although the discussion of top-slicing remains active.
17. An example of their proliferation was indicated by an advertisement for Home Box Office appearing in the *New Yorker* in January 2008. It advertised the possibility of receiving a new drama series by four different means: conventionally off-air as part of the HBO channel, streamed from the Internet, on demand or by mobile phone.
18. As a result, the BBC was fined heavily by Ofcom. Even heavier penalties were imposed by the regulator on ITV, which was required to return to their audiences millions of pounds of profits made from telephone calls charged at premium rates. For offences of a similar kind, Channel 4 was also fined heavily.
19. 'Elements of Impartiality'. An ABC Discussion Draft, November, 2007, http://www.abc.net.au/corp/pubs/documents/impartiality_sep07.pdf.
20. Section 320 (1 & 2).
21. For further information, see under Ofcom in the UK National Chapter.
22. Red Lion Broadcasting Co. Inc. v. the FCC.
23. Scott B, *We are all journalists now*, Free Press, New York, 2007, p. 172.
24. The reference is to an incident in 2005 when the veracity of a CBS News report on George Bush's National Guard service was successfully challenged by bloggers. Shortly afterwards, Dan Rather, the CBS news anchorman, gave up the evening News programme and in 2006 left the corporation, events, in some reports, not unconnected to the National Guard story.

4
National Studies

Australia

A brief history

Radio broadcasting in Australia began in 1923 when the government approved a scheme for the sale of 'sealed sets', receivers capable of picking up only one station. Enthusiasm for the new medium was mutedand the scheme was abandoned in favour of one involving alternative systems: 'A' licences funded by government-imposed licence-fees for receivers and 'B' licences dependent on advertising revenue. This time the public response was more vigorous and audience figures rose rapidly. In 1929, a new Australian Broadcasting Company, formed by a consortium of 'A' licence-holders, assumed responsibility for programming, attracting a share of licence revenues and accountable to the Postmaster-General's Department. Three years later the company was brought into public ownership as the Australian Broadcasting Commission, a title it retained for over half a century when it was given its new name, the Australian Broadcasting Corporation (ABC), under the 1983 Australian Broadcasting Corporation Act.

By the time war broke out in 1939, ABC had more than 100 radio stations scattered round the country. A similar number of commercial stations was in operation, concentrating mainly on local interests. Pressure to introduce FM broadcasting, initiated by the demand for better music services as well as a demand for services to minorities was resisted by the government until the early 1970s. Then began FM broadcasting using new UHF services. The development of community broadcasting enfranchised groups who could demonstrate a community of interests. They had to be non-profit-making and received no government funding, but could carry limited amounts of advertising.

In 1956, ABC added television to its radio services and, in Sydney and Melbourne where the Olympic Games were being staged that year, for the first time it faced commercial competition. Licences for two channels in each of the two cities had been granted to consortia formed by major newspaper groups, the forerunners of the extensive involvement of such groups in Australian broadcasting over the years. Other licences followed shortly afterwards, allowing services to be developed in Brisbane, Perth, Adelaide and Hobart. In 1963, a third licence was granted to the major cities, the government rejecting the concerns of the Australian Broadcasting Control Board, doubtful about the ability of the market to sustain it among the relatively small population. Commercial television was later extended to more than 30 regional areas where the government insisted on local ownership resisting pressure from the major commercial companies to take charge themselves. Subsequently there were mergers among the regional stations. The basic structure of large network companies with numbers of affiliates survives until today, although there have been changes in the rules of ownership.

The broadcast receiving licence was abolished in 1974, but for some years the proceeds had been paid into the Treasury and the ABC continues to be funded by a government grant, now provided on a triennial basis. For both the ABC and the Special Broadcasting Service (SBS), the next triennial review is due in the financial year 2009–2010. Intermittent efforts by industry and Parliament to force the Corporation to carry advertising or sponsorship under the description of corporate underwriting have so far proved unsuccessful.

The Green Inquiry in 1977, under the Secretary of the Posts and Telegraph Department, was charged with examining the broadcasting system as a whole. It recommended that the impending technological changes exposed the need for a more powerful regulator. As a result, the Australian Broadcasting Authority, replacing after 30 years a purely advisory Control Board, was set up in 1978. It was itself replaced under the Broadcasting Services Act of 1992 by the Australian Broadcasting Tribunal, which reflected the Government's ambition to regulate with a light touch. The Bill's language provoked the question from Paul Chadwick, then an academic, 'Are we a market rather than an audience, consumers rather than citizens?'[1]

The Green Report had recommended that the size of the then Australian Broadcasting Commission should be reduced to seven, but, under the Bill introduced late in 1977, the Government proposed to maintain the existing total of nine members. However, it also proposed to replace all nine: some before their terms of office were over. This was without precedent. The protests this provoked, inside the ABC and out, succeeded in bringing about the abandonment of the proposal and an increase in the membership of the Commission to eleven, a figure allowing the government to appoint two of its sympathisers, reducing the influence of Commissioners appointed by the previous administration which had become the Opposition.

Alex Dix was the businessman appointed in 1979, with three colleagues, to report on the ABC, following a period of turbulent relations in the wake of the Green Report: not only with the government, but also internally, diminishing the ABC's national standing. The Dix Report found that, although a high percentage of the population supported the National Broadcaster, many were dissatisfied by its performance and some sections were, in particular, critical of its failure to reflect the changing nature of Australian society. Those criticisms persisted, leading eventually in 1991 to the incorporation into statute of the SBS, 14 years after it had started radio transmissions and 11 years after its television service opened. The ABC itself had had its status as a Commission changed to that of a Corporation under a 1983 statute, having nine appointees who were called Directors to indicate a greater degree of independence. The Australian Broadcasting Tribunal was replaced in 2005 by the Australian Communications and Media Authority (ACMA), a change reflecting the need to deal with convergence within communications.

Digitalisation and the satellite era

At the end of the 1970s and into the following decade, a great deal of trouble was caused before the launch of the first Australian satellite service. The government had decided to nationalise the project under the name of Aussat and allow the ABC the use of it for extending its radio and television transmission to the furthest corners of the country. Because the government would not fund the ABC sufficiently in the view of the Commission, staff cuts were proposed. These led to a lengthy period of unrest punctuated by stoppages before the ABC service could begin in January 1986, nearly a decade after it had first been discussed. Further services were provided for in the Broadcasting Services Act, 1992.

Digitalisation began in 1971 and the process of analogue switchover is underway. The two National Broadcasters and the three free-to-air networks are committed to simultaneous analogue/digital transmissions until the process is completed in the period 2010–2012.

The legislation

There are four principal Acts of Parliament:

1. *The Australian Broadcasting Corporation Act, 1983,* which established the Corporation.
2. *The Special Broadcasting Service Act, 1991.*
3. *The Broadcasting Services Act, 1992,* under which the Australian Broadcasting Authority was set up, taking the place of the Australian Broadcasting Tribunal and introducing a regime with a lighter touch. It included a series of regulatory provisions, among them limits on ownership and respect for community standards. It designated ABC & SBS as National Broadcasters.
4. *The Australian Communications and Media Authority (ACMA) Act, 2005,* which established ACMA in place of the Australian Broadcasting Authority.

Ministerial responsibility

The name of the Department for Communications, Information Technology and the Arts was changed to the Department for Broadband, Communications and the Digital Economy on 3 December 2007. Responsibility for Culture and the Arts, including Broadcasting, passed at the same time to the Department of Environment, Water, Heritage and the Arts.

The regulator

Australian Communications and Media Authority

The Australian Communications and Media Authority succeeded the Australian Broadcasting Authority under the Australian Communications Act, 2005.

(1) *The Authority*: It consists of a Chair, a Deputy Chair and at least one other member, but no more than seven other members. They are appointed by the Governor-General for periods not exceeding five years, but may be reappointed for a period not exceeding ten years in all. Apart from the Chair and Deputy Chair, the service of the members is part-time. There is also provision for the appointment of associate members on a full-or part-time basis for a period not exceeding five years with reappointment for a total period of ten years' service.

(2) *The Authority's functions*: The Authority has responsibilities for telecommunications, spectrum management and broadcasting. Its

functions for broadcasting include the regulation of broadcasting services, Internet control and datacasting services in accordance with the Broadcasting Services Act, 1992. It allocates, renews, suspends and cancels licences and collects fees for licences. It conducts and commissions research into community attitudes on issues relating to programmes and datacasting content. It assists broadcasting service providers, sector by sector, in formulating codes of practice that, as far as possible, are in accordance with community standards, approves the codes on a triennial basis, except for the National Broadcasters, and subsequently monitors the performances of all the broadcasters. It monitors and investigates complaints concerning broadcasting (including the National Broadcasters) and datacasting services. It reports on and advises the Minister on the broadcasting industry, Internet industry and datacasting industry.

(3) *The Internet*: Since January 2000, Internet content considered offensive or illegal has been subject to a statutory scheme administered by ACMA. Established under Schedule 5 to the Broadcasting Services Act, 1992, the online content scheme evolved from a tradition of Australian content regulation in broadcasting and other entertainment media. This tradition embodies the principle that – while adults should be free to see, hear and read what they want – children should be protected from material that may be unsuitable for (or harmful to) them, and everyone should be protected from material that is highly offensive. The online content scheme seeks to achieve these objectives by a number of means such as complaint investigation processes, government and industry collaboration, and community awareness and empowerment. While administration of the scheme is the responsibility of ACMA, the principle of 'co-regulation' underpinning the scheme reflects Parliament's intention that the government, industry and community each plays a role in managing Internet safety issues in Australia. Some people strongly disagree with this approach. They say that the Australian constitution does not clearly provide either the states or the federal government with power to censor online content, so Internet censorship in Australia is typically an amalgam of various plans, laws, acts and policies. The regulator has been criticised for its role in reviewing Internet censorship in Australia and how it might be further enabled. Particular criticism has been levelled at the regulator's technical understanding of what is involved overall in Internet regulation and censorship.

(4) *Finance*: Funding is set on a rolling three-year basis. At a non-mandated time in that period, there is a capacity to have a funding

review, involving the Authority, the Department of Communications (the sponsoring department) and the Finance Department. With external accountants also involved, it is a private process to establish what the Authority has done and what that has cost and whether it has been what the government wanted. The most recent review, in 2007, resulted in an increased allocation of funding to the Authority.

The Authority retains none of its revenue from licence-fees, charges on auctions and defence, but the revenue from telecommunications regulation is subsidised by a levy on the industry. This money goes into the Consolidated Fund, out of which the Authority receives its own finances.

> It's an interesting question and one which is being discussed - whether independent funding is useful as a way of reinforcing the independence. Because I always think that in any event it depends upon where you source your revenue from. Because if you raise it directly from industry, by taxes which you then keep, or from revenue raised by, say, auctions for example, that also potentially creates a series of conflicts ... It might be conflicts [which encourage you] not to make efficiency changes which reduce revenue or to over-value, to over-plump the value of spectrum that you want to auction so that you keep a bigger share of revenue. There are conflicts both ways. And there are accountability issues with direct levies on the population.
>
> (Lyn Maddock, Deputy Chair, ACMA)

(5) *Accountability*: The Authority is required to submit an Annual Report to Parliament.

(6) *Codes of practice*: Under their members' licences from ACMA, each sector of the industry is required to submit a code of practice to the regulator who must be satisfied that the code has the support of the majority of the sector's membership and reflects community standards. Among the numerous codes currently in operation are those covering the two National Broadcasters, the commercial television and radio services, subscription services on television and radio, narrowcast radio, and community broadcasting.

In addition, ABC and SBS, both formally National Broadcasters, have their own codes, notifiable to ACMA but not requiring its approval.

The ACMA requires all complaints about alleged breaches of a code or of a licence condition to be in writing and filed initially to the responsible broadcaster. If a complaint is upheld by ACMA, its penalties extend from fines to revocation of the licence. Codes must be re-presented triennially.

(7) *Content requirements*: ACMA is able to lay down conditions in its licences for the inclusion of Australian content, programming for children, captioning, expenditure on drama production and the provision of classification symbols and statements when drama or feature films are being screened. It maintains an 'anti-siphoning' agreement to restrict exclusive arrangements for the screening of popular sporting events. The recent Free Trade Agreement with the US has raised questions about the continuation of the requirements for Australian content, a difficulty compounded by the extensive reliance on popular American material in Australian programme schedules. It also requires the classification of films in accordance with the rules of the Classification Board which cover a wide range of media outlets. Classification is as follows: G for General; PG for Parental Guidance Recommended; M for Mature Audiences. The rest are legally enforceable: MA for 15 and above, under-15s to be accompanied; R for 18 and above; X for 18 and above, where there is sexually explicit material. The classification has to be shown at the time of transmission.

National Broadcasters

Australian Broadcasting Corporation

The Australian Broadcasting Corporation (ABC) succeeded the Australian Broadcasting Commission under the Australian Broadcasting Act, 1983, and was later identified as a National Broadcaster.

(1) *The Board* consists of the Managing Director and not less than five and not more than seven non-executive directors appointed by the Governor-General. Non-executive directors serve for a period of five years, but may be re-appointed. The Board appoints the Managing Director for a period of five years and he/she may be appointed for a further period of five years. The Governor-General appoints the Chair and Deputy Chair from among the non-executive directors who must be experienced in broadcasting services or communications or management, having expertise in financial or technical matters or having cultural or other interests which the Governor-General considers relevant to the oversight of a public broadcasting organisation. Apart from the Chair and Deputy Chair, the service of the appointees is part-time.

(2) *Programme Services*: The Charter of the ABC appears as Section 6 of the Act, reproduced in Appendix i. The Corporation is responsible for the following:

Television
An Analogue Television service.
Digital television from 177 transmitters(simulcast with analogue TV).
ABC2, a second digital channel started in 2005.
Local television in each state and territory.
Under contract with the Department of Foreign Affairs and Trade, Australia Network, an international service, broadcasts via satellite and rebroadcasts to 41 countries in the Asia-Pacific region.

Radio
Four national radio networks: Radio National, ABC Classic, Triple 3 and ABC News Radio.
Local radio – nine metropolitan stations and 51 regional stations.
Three Internet music-based services.
Radio Australia, an international service carried on shortwave, Internet, and satellite and local rebroadcasts in five local languages. Government operated between 1944–50.

Internet
ABC Online was launched in 1995 and, described by defenders as a vital national resource, has survived attempts to force it into partnership with commercial interests.

(3) *Advisory Councils and Committees*: The Board has the duty of appointing an ABC Advisory Council. In making appointments to the Council the Board must have regard to the desirability of including representatives of the Australian community. The Council may be consulted by the Board or raise issues on their own initiative. The Board may appoint additional advisory councils in any state, territory or region. These may be consulted by the ABC Advisory Council about matters concerning the areas of their respective responsibilities. They may also themselves raise such matters with the ABC Advisory Council.

(4) *Standards*: The Corporation must take account of the standards determined from time to time by the ACMA in respect of the broadcasting services. It must produce a code of practice which is notified to ACMA, but, as a statutory body unlike the commercial operators, does not need ACMA's approval.

(5) *Finance*: The ABC receives funding from parliamentary grants (A$862.7 million in 2006–2007). In addition, it receives income from the sale of goods and services.

(6) *Ministerial Direction*: The Minister responsible for broadcasting may direct the broadcasting of a particular matter if he/she considers it to be of national interest and the Corporation must broadcast the matter over all of its national broadcasting services or over such of them as are specified in the direction. The broadcast must be made free of charge, but the Corporation may state that the broadcast is taking place in accordance with a directive. Similarly, the Corporation may state when it has been directed to withdraw material from transmission.

(7) *Accountability*: The Corporation is required to present an annual report to Parliament. It may be called to give evidence to Committees of the Senate or the House of Representatives on relevant issues.

Special Broadcasting Service

The Special Broadcasting Service (SBS) was incorporated under the Special Broadcasting Service Act, 1991 and later identified as a National Broadcaster.

(1) *The Board* consists of no fewer than four and no more than eight non-executive directors appointed by the Governor-General and is responsible for the appointment of the Managing Director who is also a Board member. The Governor-General has to be satisfied that one non-executive director has an appropriate understanding of the interests of employees.

(2) *Functions*: Section 6 of the Act contains the Charter of the SBS reproduced in Appendix ii.

(3) *Advisory Committee*: The Board is required to create a Community Advisory Committee (CAC) to advise it on community needs and opinions, including those of small or newly arrived ethnic groups, on matters relevant to the Charter. Persons appointed to the CAC must have an understanding of Australia's multicultural society, and, in particular, have interests relevant to, and an understanding of, ethnic, Aboriginal or Torres Strait Islander communities.

> It is very much a public broadcaster entity.... it's a committee, with a maximum of 14 but the Board likes it to be around 12. There are two Board members who sit on it and it's supported by management as a secretariat.... It doesn't have any sort of binding (authority). It

can't pass a resolution that requires the Corporation or the Board to do anything. It is an advisory body, not a deliberative body. It meets 3 times a year and has a very wide agenda.... the Minister asked us to think about how we could go about (improving the communication of the public broadcasters).So what we're looking at now, we're looking at the mechanics of it, is that within the websites there will be an ability for members of the public to see what's on the CAC agenda, email comments in prior to the meeting and get some level of comment back as to what the CAC meeting discussed.... you don't want to create this idea of an organisation with, if you like, a mandate. The body is representative of the community in the sense that it's selected from a broad cross section. It's not representative in the sense that it is elected or empowered.... So getting that sort of balance right can be quite difficult.

(Bruce Meagher, Director of Strategy and Communications, SBS)

(4) *Standards*: The Act requires the Service to have a code of practice which, like that of the other National Broadcaster, the ABC, does not have to be approved by ACMA, but is notified to the Authority which is empowered to monitor the SBS's performance.

(5) *Finance*: The SBS receives funding from a parliamentary appropriation on a triennial basis. It also receives revenue from advertising and from sponsorship. Advertising is limited to five minutes each hour and can appear between programmes or in natural breaks. It is also allowed under certain conditions to benefit from product placement, although the new SBS Code of Practice has been the subject of controversy.

(6) *Ministerial Direction*: If the Minister is of the opinion that the broadcasting of particular matter by the Corporation would be in the national interest, the Minister may direct the Corporation to broadcast that matter over all of its national broadcasting services or over such of them as are specified in the direction. If such a direction is given, the Corporation must broadcast that matter, free of charge, in accordance with the direction. The Minister may also indicate the language to be used. The Corporation may indicate that it is acting in response to a Ministerial directive.

(7) *Accountability*: The SBS is required to present an annual report to Parliament and to give evidence to select committees from the Senate or the House of Representatives.

Non-commercial broadcasters

The Community Broadcasting Association of Australia

(1) *Community Broadcasting*: This has been licensed since 1992, but permanent, continuous, licensing did not begin for another two years. The Community Broadcasting Association of Australia (CBAA) is composed of individual not-for-profit organisations who can demonstrate to the regulator a community of interests which justifies a licence. Thus, in heavily populated areas, such a community may be identified, for example, by age, religious belief or particular ethnicity. Outside the major centres, the licensed services are characterised by clusters of interests – sports, recreational activities, geographical. The services must be compatible with reception on easily available equipment. There is an expectation in Section 2 of the Broadcasting Standards Act, 1992 that members of the community should have opportunities for participation in the operations and the programme decisions of the stations. The conduct of the stations is governed by an ACMA-registered Code of Practice. In preparation for the triennial renewal of the Code, extensive consultations take place on a national basis, involving the individual licensees, the public and public interest groups.

(2) *Funding*: In May 2007, the government granted A$10.1 million for capital and operations and planning and co-ordination over four years, but no provision was made for content. Funding may also come from individual states or from local communities, as well as members' subscriptions. No government funding has yet been allowed for community television, although it is available for radio, but it may sell blocks of airtime to third party not-for-profit interests or to higher education institutions. There is often feuding between the parties on the borderline between commercial television and community broadcasting. Some community television services, notably those in Perth and Melbourne, have reputedly been successful in raising state funds, sponsorship and donations from educational institutions.

(3) *Technical*: There is no distinction in signal strength between community broadcasters and other services. On 1 January 2009, Eureka 147 becomes the platform for digital radio. Digital is intended to be a supplementary service, so that analogue listeners are not abandoned. In the state capitals, some 40 stations are eligible for admission to the first stage of digitalisation and it is expected that most will take the opportunity to expand their services. They will no longer retain their own transmission facilities, but will be sharing multiplexes with the commercial radio

industry. It is anticipated that they will together form joint-venture companies to own and operate the digital facilities. At the time of writing, community television has not been told when it might have an allocation of digital frequencies. The movement of the public towards digital take-up has meant a steady erosion in the take-up of the analogue Community Television services and an increasingly critical loss of revenue. With the coming of digital, the stations will lose their ownership of spectrum and will have to form coalitions to find places on the new platforms.

Commercial broadcasters

Commercial television: Free TV

There are three national commercial television networks: Seven Network, Nine Network and Network Ten. In addition, there are regional television networks, often carrying programmes from one or other of the national networks. ACMA has the power to decide on the number of major networks serving any one region and may limit it to one where the revenue is limited or may allow a single company to own and operate two channels. Conditions, described in more detail below, are attached to licences, prescribing, for example, local origination, programmes for children or the use of Australian-produced programmes.

The sector's code of practice calls for fairness, accuracy and a respect for privacy in news.

Advertising on television is the responsibility of the Advertising Standards Bureau, which administers a national self-regulatory scheme under a code of ethics with which advertisers must comply. The code is drawn up by the Association of National Advertisers working to principles agreed by Parliament.

National Indigenous Television

Supported by the Backing Indigenous Ability initiative, National Indigenous Television (NITV) was launched on 13 July 2007 as a company limited by guarantee. Although sometimes described as a National Broadcaster, it neither has the statutory status of ABC or SBS nor is it a broadcaster, it is a content provider and its programmes are distributed nationally through other broadcasting services.

(1) *Functions*: NITV commissions, produces and brings together indigenous television content, including indigenous news, documentaries, drama, children's programmes, sport and other genres; informing,

entertaining and educating indigenous and other audiences about Australia's indigenous people, their customs and issues. It seeks its audiences primarily from among indigenous people, but also from the public at large.

(2) *Technical*: Its programmes are delivered as a dedicated channel via Imparja Television's narrowcast service and directly received in homes as well as terrestrial re-transmission through 160 Remote Indigenous Broadcasting Services (RIBS) sites. It is also available on two pay TV platforms, Foxtel and Austar.

(3) *Standards*: Responsibility for compliance rests with the individual broadcasters transmitting NITV's programmes. They in turn have to comply with the relevant codes of practice: in the case of Foxtel and Austar, that is the ASTRA Code for Open Narrowcast Television, and in the case of Imparja Television, it is ASTRA's Code of Practice for Subscription Broadcast Television Code. For ASTRA, see 'Subscription Television' below.

(4) *Funding*: Before its first programmes went on air in June 2007, the Australian government agreed to pay NITV A$48.5 million over four years ending in June 2010. In addition, it has revenue from advertising and sponsorship.

Subscription television

The Australian Satellite Television and Radio Association (ASTRA) was formed in 1997, five years after the introduction of satellite television under the Broadcasting Services Act, 1992. It represents satellite services, narrowcast television services, programme channel providers, subscription television operators and communications companies and other associate members. It has the duty to develop the codes of practice for the different services it represents. These include the platform owners who hold licences from ACMA. Among them are Foxtel, Optus and Austar which is mainly directed to remote Australia. Members also include numerous channels providing programmes for the platforms, including CNBC, BBC World and Satellite Music Australia. Associate members include the providers of equipment or services such as legal advice. The Association's Board consists of six members from the major platforms and six representing the channels and the associate members. Subscription television is now entirely digitalised. There is a requirement to classify films and drama in accordance with the Office of Film and Literature's guidelines. In addition to a local content requirement, the Association is obliged to preface some programmes with messages about their content – for instance, violence or drug-taking. The Association has embarked on a step-by-step programme of close captioning across all programmes, volunteering to do so as a potentially valuable part of its services and, as Debra Richards, CEO of ASTRA, explained, anticipating official pressure to do so,

> at the end of the first 5 years, the first 20 channels will be required to be at 25 percent [of programmes captioned] and the next 20 channels, will be at 15 percent. Interestingly, a number of our movie channels are already at 65 percent because once you start captioning, it reduces the costs, you begin to build up a library, all those sort of things.... We think we ought to do this rather than being 'required' to do it. We think we should be on the front foot. We also see this is a great marketing tool, and it can become an incentive for subscriber take-up and in turn can benefit subscribers in the community.... So there is a public interest.

There are obligations on members to fund drama output at the same level as free-to-air (commercial) television does, but not necessarily to transmit it. The annual contribution made to the audio-visual industry was estimated by Debra Richards as about A$20 million. She said that there were no obligations on ASTRA's members to transmit Australian material. On the other hand, without Australian material they would have no subscribers. The demand from the audience across the whole range of Australian broadcasting for Australian programming is one of its most characteristic features, with Australian programmes typically dominating the Top Twenty. Subscribers to satellite services pay about A$40 a month for the smallest bundle of services and A$110 for the highest level.

Engagement with the public

To the consideration of the broadcasters' accountability to Parliament, regulators or, in the case of commercial operators, shareholders and advertisers, it is necessary to add the daily processes of accountability to the public. They can take one of three forms: grievances and complaints, consultations and group-lobbying. The first of them are delivered in different forms: either online or by telephone and mail. Their volume, even at its highest, is invariably small in comparison with the size of the audience watching at any time. Murray Green, Director of Corporate Strategy and Governance, described how complaints were handled by ABC:

If somebody complains about any of our content that complaint is not assessed by the people who produced that content but goes to an independent unit within the organisation called Audience and Consumer Affairs, some of whom are former journalists, led by someone who has come from the Ombudsman's office, so there is a real professional approach to complaint handling. We are dealing with about 40,000 contacts a year, over half of which are written. The written ones all get individual responses. And so, what happens is that the Audience and Consumer Affairs group, which is independent of any content area, will come to an independent assessment of the person who has complained, the nature of the complaint, whether the complaint is upheld or not. If the complaint is not upheld, the person who has complained has the opportunity of two avenues of review: they can seek a review from the internal Ombudsman, the Complaints Review Executive, and he will start again with the complaint, look at what the ABC has said and the nature of the person's enduring concern and come up with a view. If they are still unhappy, they can go to the Independent Complaints Review Panel, which is a panel that has been appointed by the ABC Board headed by a retired Supreme Court judge and the convenor. The judge is appointed by the Board but the other two members are nominated by the St James Ethics Centre and the Communications Law Centre. What they do is provide a list from which the Board chooses and that's the process of appointment. And if a person is still unhappy they can go off to the external regulator, ACMA.... I think we're engaging at a far more serious level than we've ever engaged before. Not to say that we treated matters frivolously but there's a lot of work that goes into consideration of somebody's complaint and all those complaints, the ones that are upheld, are reported to the Board and we publish every quarter all the upheld complaints that have been sustained on our website so people can see what complaints have been upheld.

Interviewer: So it means people can make fact-based criticism – sometimes an innovative concept in Australian public life [laughter].

Jock Given, Professor of Media and Communications, Swinburne Institute of Social Research at Melbourne University, offered his own explanation:

> I think there's quite a lot of engagement but it varies a lot across different issues. I think the complaints process is the obvious place where much of that can occur... but there are particularly celebrated incidents where media gets quite involved as well, where there's quite a lot of attention around. An example of this would be sexual activity on *Big Brother*: the so-called 'turkey slapping' incident which becomes the topic of talkback radio, lots of media attention and there is a sort of complaints and regulatory process involved where much of what happens seems to be played out in the media.[2] There is also scope for research and I think perhaps the regulator is encouraged to undertake research about matters which are of concern to the public. I think my sense overall is perhaps that the big transition that happened in Australian broadcasting regulation 15 years ago [the 1992 Broadcasting Services Act] which was supposedly to encourage a much more lively research agenda, a shift from a system which relied entirely on complaints and therefore seen as privileging particular individuals or particular lobby groups who might make a fuss about particular issues which were not necessarily as sensitive to the whole population. The idea was that it would become much more based upon research, so that we would find out what the whole community thought, not just people who were prepared to make complaints. My sense is that hasn't really happened because there has been a reluctance to investigate too deeply issues which may be politically contentious or that might uncover unpalatable facts. I think one of the most important of those related to the effect of ownership rationalization and networking in the commercial radio industry and its impact on local programmes in country areas. I think that issue was a very live issue for a long time before official policy/regulatory scrutiny was directed to it. I think people cared a lot about it, I think local politicians knew a lot about it well before... Eventually, some rules were put in place, some requirements for coverage of matters of local interest.

Mark Armstrong, former Chair of ABC, was asked how active were the Australian public, advocacy groups and even the regulator in expressing concerns about the merits of television programmes. In answering, he expressed the view that opportunities for public involvement had declined:

> I'm not sure what the measure is but I would say they're much less active than they were 20 years ago and the main reason for that is they don't have the opportunity to make any constructive input as distinct from making complaints. To talk about serious public contribution in relation to TV programming, we have to go back really a couple of decades because that's how long ago there was a lot of serious input, in my opinion. I think the point in time we look at would be 1976 and '77: 1976 having seen the Green Report, which was a fresh look at broadcasting regulation, Green having been Secretary of the relevant government department (see p. 79). It put a lot of emphasis on accountability in relation to programmes and also in relation to planning and technical issues which the public care a lot about when it comes to reception and the choices they're offered. And that was followed in 1976 and '77 by legislation which established the Australian Broadcasting Tribunal and a system of public accountability and review. All the years since 1977 in my opinion have consisted of cutting back on useful or positive ways for the public to contribute and the relegation of the public input to complaints, which in my experience, and I was a full-time member of the ABT for 5 years, is not what most of the public want to speak about . . . They want to talk about what kinds of programmes they receive and what kind of channels. They do want to talk about children's television and how it is presented and the extent to which that's associated with advertising and the extent to which it's relevant to Australian children or Australian made. All the surveys that I used to see said that the public wanted more documentary type programming, more local documentary programmes and there were even bigger trends such as the question of local drama production. These are not issues where the public is offered much opportunity to contribute to these days.

Did Mark Armstrong believe that there was real public engagement with ACMA on issues like reality television or the enquiry just announced on the sexualisation of children? Were they more about people complaining than having the opportunity to contribute constructively?

> Well, I'd like to hear how the public can contribute constructively anymore. I don't see an avenue. If we take the issue you mentioned

about the ACMA investigation of offensive material on reality TV such as *Big Brother*.My understanding is there has been very little public input or concern about that issue and the surveys have tended to show that the public are not very concerned about *Big Brother* -type programmes, at least not very concerned about the excesses beyond general community standards at the moment that have been involved. To me, those issues are squarely within the traditional game as it's been played for about 50 years of micro adjustments to community standards and all of the theatre and symbolic politics that surrounds breaches and alleged breaches, particularly loved by politicians in marginal electorates who can make very good use for their own selfish purposes of finding a few community complaints and getting some publicity which they otherwise find it difficult to find.

When she was commenting on a suggestion that indifference among the public was a factor in the decline in the numbers of complaints, Lyn Maddock of ACMA said that it was not a reflection of apathy. It was, she believed, that one of the characteristics of the Australian community was a capacity not to bother about what you do not think is very important. She asked what genuine public opinion was:

What is public opinion? If you take what our surveys, focus groups, and complaints have shown the mass of the populace thinks, then we were pretty much in touch with what they were thinking. If you take it as to what those who comment in public wanted, we were often seen as out of touch, but we made sure at the time of our review that we did quality research, we did general surveys, we had focus groups, we looked at ratings and we had the legitimate complaints to us. And I think most people weren't concerned.

Interviewer: Weren't concerned?

Maddock: We explored whether people have seen anything on television in the last twelve months, which had concerned them. We followed that up – if they had, it was often in the news. When we asked whether they had seen too much sexual content, and if so, when did you see it – if they had, they often cited *Home and Away* and *Neighbours*. And when we asked who they thought should make decisions about what was shown on television, 91 percent said they wanted to themselves. This is in the context of a 'code of practice' basis to regulating content on television in which public consultation is mandated and the television networks have to document to us how they have dealt with the issues raised and, if they have rejected suggestions, why they have. So, on an assessment that the codes incorporate the public mood fairly accurately and the views about who should make decisions on what is shown on TV, the outcome of a low level of concern about individual cases is not unexpected.

Grievances and complaints

ACMA does not accept complaints about the quality or scheduling of programmes, the content of advertisements, advertising on SBS or alleged advertising on ABC. Complaints alleging a breach of the broadcaster's licence may be directed to the regulator, but complaints laid against alleged breaches of a broadcaster's code of practice have to be first directed to the broadcaster involved. However, there is a developing tendency for complainants to allege licence breaches which then have to be investigated by ACMA. If a broadcaster fails to reply to a complaint within 60 days, ACMA will take action to secure a response. At ABC

> we have 40,000 contacts a year of which about just over half are written and the written complaints all get written responses. There's a very active interaction.
>
> (Murray Green, ABC)

Andrew Stewart, a solicitor practising media law, recalled a particular complaint, relatively rare in going the distance to the courts:

> Probably the most significant thing that I was involved in was complaints about a *60 Minutes* programme which depicted Russell Crowe [an Australian actor] smoking. Any depiction of cigarette smoking usually generates a reasonable number of complaints and this one generated complaints from that first category of people who merely didn't like it but also quite a few complaints from various advocacy groups. And I think that the one that ended up going to ACMA was by one of the media groups that represents the interests of youth and they complained to ACMA. ACMA found a breach of the broadcaster's licence because broadcasters have to comply with all laws and there are prohibitions on tobacco advertising. The broadcaster appealed to the Federal Court on the basis that the appearance of the cigarettes was incidental to the interview, but that wasn't ultimately accepted by the Federal Court.

Barry Melville, General Manager of the CBAA, gave an example of another kind of complaint alleging a breach of licence.

... disgruntled volunteers in stations, alleging that they've been denied the opportunity to fully participate or democratically contribute to services as is set out in Schedule 2 of the BSA and bringing on complaints that, in many cases, may border on vexatious or they're people with an axe to grind. How closely that relates to genuine grievances on behalf of wider audiences is a moot point.

Were complainants satisfied with their treatment?

Sometimes all that people want to do is vent about something which is fine, they can write to us or phone or make a formal complaint A lot of the people that use the formal complaints process do so because they have a particular perception of what they perceive to be bias based upon their particular stance on an issue. The biggest one we've had going in the last few years is this whole issue of the Armenian genocide and the Turkish community objecting to a particular documentary. Our view of that is largely that the documentary itself was a reasonable documentary, it had a point of view but that's perfectly legitimate and that there wasn't a basis to object to that documentary as such. We come under quite a bit of pressure around issues in the Middle East, they're hugely contentious so we get lots of complaints based around that. I think complainants think the process is good or bad depending on whether we agree with their complaint. I suppose the testing thing is that very few complaints, even where we dismiss them, very few are proceeded with to ACMA, the regulator, only a tiny number.(Even though) there's no cost to them, they don't have to engage lawyers. In no way is it onerous and obviously we are very open about that. So I suppose if there's a test that's probably the best one that we can apply.

(Bruce Meagher, Director of Communications and Strategy, SBS)

Consultations

Its General Manager, Barry Melville, described how the Community Broadcasters Association conducted consultation with its members:

Starting at a national level, CBAA, every 3–5 years, have a nationally oriented consultation process around code of practice review/code of practice development, depending on what stage in the cycle we're at. They are by no means voluntary codes – they're called self-regulatory codes, but they become mandatory and they're registered with ACMA – and there is a negotiation process with ACMA. So we undertake a consultative process that involves licensees – community broadcasting stations – but as an extension of that, we also place notices and invite members of the public and public interest groups to also comment on the adequacy or otherwise of the code frameworks. There's a code for community television and there's a code for community radio ... (We don't get) a lot of feedback from the public. We get a lot from community broadcasters – placing that qualifier that there's obviously an overlap between voluntary broadcasters and the public, that they are a particular, motivated, already participating interest group.

Interviewer: It's interesting because similarly in the public broadcasting sector, where they also advertise for opinions, the number of people who are actually motivated is small, but there are certain groups ....

Melville: Yes, but statistically insignificant if you are trying to actually survey the efficacy or adequacy of a proposal. But that doesn't seem to be the point.

Interviewer: They're voices, it's a democratic process.

Melville: It's open, it's democratic. At the station level, there's no inherent requirement that they undertake community consultation in any particular way except they must maintain governance structures that are open and participatory so again I guess I must admit it smacks of the self selecting, but the more motivating members of the public who wish to have some say or some effect at some level can join the association at one level. At another level, they can choose to become a volunteer and participant either in administration, production or on air presentation, and the third tier obviously is that they can seek to become involved through the association in governance. They can seek to be selected for a board or committee of management. So, it's the very act of participation in community media that defines the level of public input.

Bridget Fair of Seven Network told of her company's handling of the triennial Code Review.

We put out a draft code for comment. We're required to review our code every three years and we're coming up to a code review now.

The process works this way: we go talk to the regulator about what we're thinking of changing, we have an informal chat about those things and we then put out a draft code for comment and we advertise that in various newspapers and there's a consultation period. We put a whole lot of information on websites and so forth and people write in and tell us their views on the various aspects of the code that's changed. We usually put out an explanatory document; we don't just put out a changed code. We tell people where the changes are.

Interviewer: How many people are likely to write to such a review?

Fair: Last time we had 1,100 responses, which is a pretty big response. Most Senate Committees and so forth wouldn't get that many responses.

Interviewer: I've noticed recent ads in the metropolitan papers.

Fair: We always advertise changes to the code because they're required to be the subject of public consultation under the Act anyway. ACMA is required to consult and ensure things meet community standards. We advertise our own code and its complaint processes on television and we are required to do that under the code. Then, when we come to the Code Review, we advertise those in the press and that's generally the way Senate Committees and other formal processes work and we do the same.

Quid pro quo: The obligations of commercial broadcasters

Although the obligations imposed on the commercial television licensees might not be acknowledged as recognition of a public interest in broadcasting, they are nevertheless designed to ensure that the output of the stations should contribute to the public interest: economically as a stimulus for the Australian broadcasting industry, socially as a concern for the interests of children and a regard for minorities and culturally as an encouragement to Australian creativity. However, in the case of the Free Trade Agreement negotiated with the US in 2004, the Australian government had to give up its freedom to protect Australian content of the kind described by Jock Given earlier. He discussed the consequences:

On the Australian content question, this has obviously been one of the crucial questions that people have to engage with in the Free Trade Agreement with the United States. Because trade agreements generally, but especially that one, because the US is the country we were doing the deal with, and it is the most important source of audio-visual programmes for free-to-air television, pay television, the cinema industry, the music industry, etc. So, the extent to which Australia constrained its ability to introduce, maintain and adopt new policies in future in that Agreement was really a crucial step for us. So when we sat down to look at that [free trade] Agreement, we had to make decisions about whether we wanted to retain the capacity to use all those sorts of instruments in the future and, if we were, were we prepared to place any constraints around them? Well the answer was, we did place some constraints around them. The detail of it, you'll still get some disagreements about what it means. Our capacity to use tax schemes was reasonably well maintained. The main area where we have constrained ourselves is in relation to quotas and they've been very important to us in the past. The judgment was, I guess, some saying even if you think quotas were a useful and appropriate policy instrument in the past, they will not be useful and appropriate policy instrument in the future. We have chosen to constrain ourselves in ways we didn't need to do, I think responding to both of those arguments, that we will be less able to impose these in the future and they will not be as good a device for regulating the media industries of the future. If there are more players providing content than in an environment of three commercial networks and two public service networks, then the idea of requiring any one of them to transmit certain amounts of Australian content will not be an appropriate way to regulate them.

Bridget Fair of Seven Network described the working out of another of the obligations incurred by her company:

Under the Broadcasting Services Act, 1992, we have a requirement to contribute to adequate and comprehensive services. That is not a requirement to produce every item in a comprehensive service. The triennial process of revising the sector's code of practice in consultation with ACMA is the place where the regulator may exert pressure to change an emphasis in the code. A few years ago violence was a big concern and the regulator was conducting a lot of community research about what people thought about that, and feeding that into News and Current Affairs and people were worried about people seeing 9/11 footage and their children watching that sort of stuff. Now, it's much more about sex, because we're much more in this socially conservative phase with the community and we've got politicians who hold the balance of power who represent essentially the Christian Right. That is being reflected in things like the Minister recently announcing that there would be a review of the sexualisation of children on free-to-air television, even though the complaints that had generated that concern were really about Internet magazines. But it's always much easier to regulate us because they have the power to do so.

An enquiry into reality TV had recommended that a more onerous test should be applied to the Mature Audiences classification (MA), restricted to people over 15:

> ... and introducing a whole new type of classification test that's never been heard of anywhere else in the world which is, essentially, devised to placate people who have strong religious views about not wanting to see certain things on TV even though they're only shown after 9 o'clock at night and have to accord with strict classification requirements anyway. Generally speaking, free-to-air broadcasters know that their position of privilege, if you want to describe it that way, depends on there being large community support, so you do calibrate what you put on TV according to that view – that's one way of looking at it as a responsibility. Again, ultimately it plays out in ratings. If you don't show things that people approve of, ultimately they won't watch your channel.

Viewed widely as being of particular importance are the obligations towards children. Following is the view of Jenny Buckland, a lawyer, who has been CEO of the Australian Children's Television Foundation for the past six years:

> I don't think that broadcasters themselves necessarily accept that 'public interest' term. You know, in the UK, public service broadcasting doesn't just mean the BBC – it means ITV, Channel 4, the public service obligations those broadcasters have. Here they talk about regulation, but they don't necessarily equate it with public interest standards in terms of watershed hours, what they show where and when, being aware during the day that a younger audience is watching and perhaps late at night. All of those things. Perhaps an obligation to reflect our community, our identity but also not to broadcast things that are offensive, that vilify people, that kind of thing.

She was asked to define where the public interest lay in children's programmes:

> Well, we think that's about citizenship and about cultural identity and about real engagement with what goes on the screen. Our experience has been that when children – it doesn't mean that children don't enjoy lots of things from around the world – but when children are exposed to their own culture and get to see that, that's quite exciting for them. It's like any of us watching a film that's set in our neighbourhood: you get quite excited by it but you also develop a sense and a questioning about your community and your culture and nation that, if you're not exposed to any of that, it's almost as though you're a backwater, you're a second-class place. So we think that's really critical. But we also think it's critical to explore a wide range of issues that are relevant to the audience and fun for the audience but that may not particularly travel or be what you see when you see programmes for other countries. A lot of children that we've interviewed, when they comment about American television, they talk about how different the lifestyle is there, that American shows focus a lot on dating and shopping and things that perhaps aren't ordinary actually for an Australian teenager to the same extent – we live a different kind of lifestyle. There's also again, not to want to single out American programmes, but they're all really beautiful in American programmes and that's not the way life is and it is not a great media image if you're coming home every day and everyone on television is blonde and blue eyed and absolutely perfect and has an unlimited amount of money to be out swanning around the shopping mall after school. Kids enjoy seeing a wider range of things than that. So we think that that's really really important.

Debra Richards, CEO of ASTRA, said that among the obligations laid on the Association's members was a requirement that they contributed an annual sum to Australian production, although there was no corresponding requirement to show the results on the screen. They were also required to have their drama and films classified and had also given an undertaking eventually to caption all their output, with the exception of live sport. They are also obliged under their code to offer subscribers a lock-out facility so that they can block material they do not want to watch.

What was the future of content regulation in the face of a proliferation of channels? Bridget Fair replied,

I think there will be increasing pressure for change but not on the moral side of things. I think that in terms of what broadcasters are required to do morally, I'll be retired before I see anyone suggesting we have more relaxed rules about when we can show M programming or MA programming and breasts on television. All that sort of stuff I don't see in future changing much. I think people are becoming more conservative in that way and I think as long as broadcasters continue to occupy a very prominent position in the media landscape, there will be higher expectations on them and it's just a historical fact. People have that expectation and something that's free, that they expect they're entitled to, they also expect higher standards from, whether that's reasonable or not. We're in a situation now where, even though pay TV viewership is growing and across an entire day, probably in a pay TV household, more than half the entire viewing in that household is of pay TV channels, which are much less regulated than free-to-air channels. But when you get to prime time, which is when the majority of people are watching television, between 80 and 90 percent of viewing of TV in all homes is still of free-to-air television. And, as long as free to air is in that dominant position of the things that everyone's watching, the rules about what we have to show will continue – in terms of those moral kind of issues. In terms of other issues, like Australian content and things that are much more financial, I think when more spectrum becomes available on analogue switch-off, there will be a wholesale reconsideration of some of those requirements. We pay 9 percent of gross revenue in licence-fees. We have to broadcast 55 percent of Australian content, we have to broadcast specified amounts of drama, children's programming and we can't broadcast more than 20 percent of foreign commercials. Those kinds of imposts on broadcasters will, I think, be relaxed. I don't think they'll ever disappear. Anti-siphoning (a ban on exclusive coverage of major sporting events) will probably come under pressure. The higher the penetration of pay television, the greater the pressure on the anti-siphoning list rules. A lot of the debate around those kinds of issues is very emotional. The idea that you can't sit down with your dad and watch the New Year's Day cricket test unless you pay $100 per month is still quite, not terribly palatable to many Australians. If there's one issue in this portfolio that's a vote changer, not having access to your favourite sports is that issue.

Interviewer: It's a very interesting incarnation of the public interest... It is probably one of those few ones where what's interesting to the public coincides with the public interest. As opposed to something that is good for, or worthy.

Lyn Maddock, Deputy Chair of ACMA, looked forward to a major review of the options:

We shall have a big review at the end of next year [2008] or shortly after. This will need to, amongst other things, look at the requirements that there are on the commercial public free-to-air sector. Because of concerns both about whether they are appropriate in the new multi-channel environment and, secondly, whether in practical sense compliance is enforceable. Traditionally, as a country, we have had the view that there should definitely be an obligation to have local content in various forms and various genres. We also have a view that there should be – in the way we have structured the whole industry – very wide geographic coverage. And subscription broadcasting also has a local content obligation, achieved in their case through an expenditure obligation rather than a must-show obligation. Questions are arising as to whether these types of obligations are sustainable in the future. And if the content obligation cannot be sustainably linked to the transmission obligation, you come fairly quickly to a New Zealand type model with efforts being made to ensure that content is accessible, that it doesn't get lost in a cacophony of the Internet, multiple broadcast channels etc. Because if you are interested in ensuring that Australian content – in our case – is available to people, then a raft of new approaches and new platforms can be used. The timetable is uncertain, the direction of change seems less so.

The future for the National Broadcasters: Funding

Alongside questions about the future of content regulation within commercial television, there are questions about the future role of the two National Broadcasters, ABC and SBS, and, closely linked, the issue of public funding. In the interview Mark Armstrong, former Chair of ABC, gave for this book, he suggested that the ABC should not duplicate sports coverage which was being provided by commercial free-to-air channels or, in the longer term when it had gained more subscribers, by pay TV. Bridget Fair of Seven Network, quoted above, believed that many Australians would resist the idea that pay TV should be allowed exclusive coverage of such events, denying less-affluent viewers their chance to participate. Bruce Meagher, of SBS, thought that the role of the National Broadcasters would grow in importance.

If you're looking at more expensive genres of programming, potentially it will become increasingly difficult to create that sort of programming, certainly local programming. So, the fact of (public funding) at least gives you an underpinning of financial support to make some of that. Now the grim reality is of course that public funding isn't increasing so that it is going to be a real challenge. How you do that. And I think there's going to be some quite interesting and difficult choices to be made.... What it is you want to achieve. There are so many things you can do and there's this expectation particularly in the online world of creating so much content. But how much of it is really valuable, would you be better focusing on a more limited range of things and doing them well, in an environment where other people are... When I was talking to a guy from the BBC recently he was saying they're doing a major review of their websites and trying really seriously to ask the question 'does every single bit of television content have (to have) a Rolls Royce website backing it up' and all the other websites, who is actually looking at these things?... The BBC is grappling at the moment with the whole issue of catch-up TV but geographically barring people from getting access to certain content but whether that model, is why wouldn't they say let people download and purchase it direct from us.

Interviewer: And that's an interesting issue the ABC has been grappling with... Because a public broadcaster traditionally provides things for free.

Meagher: Yes. As are we. And I suspect we're going to go to the model: there's a catch up period, a free catch-up period and then after that if you want to rent or to own, there's a payment and that's not out of step with the sort of DVD model which now seems perfectly reasonable. But nonetheless because it's a public good, if people are not going to watch your broadcast stream, they should have the opportunity to acquire it as a public good.

For the future

Two strands of thought ran through many of the Australian interviews. The first was the need to draw together the many different ethnic groups which have gathered in the country, particularly since the end of the Second World War. This has been acknowledged in the drive towards universality of coverage, a basic principle of public service broadcasting extended by a government decision to the commercial sectors. The second is a corollary of the first, the emphasis placed on the provision of local material across a range of genres, including drama. The policy has had cultural effects, but there have been economic effects too. In the development of a production industry, it has not only served the domestic market, but also had results in markets overseas. On the evidence of the interviews, the two priorities are going to persist. However, the provision of locally originated material faces two difficulties. The Free Trade Agreement with the US led to concessions by Australia which will limit some aspects of the policy. At the same time, there are constraints which the end of spectrum scarcity and an increase in competition impose on Australian regulators as they do on regulatory bodies elsewhere.

One partial solution briefly touched on in the interviews was the introduction of transferable obligations, an idea canvassed with some vigour among the broadcasters at one time. It would mean that those obligations which could realistically survive might be spread across the industry, sector by sector, so that, taken together, they might serve the public need.

In considering the extent to which commercial broadcasters would reduce their overall local origination, several of the interviewees gave evidence of the considerable popularity of such material. Its disappearance from the schedules would be reflected unfavourably in the viewing figures.

In a situation of economic uncertainty, the role of the National Broadcasters gains in significance if the two policy objectives described in the opening paragraph of this section are to be achieved. Their state funding, as long as it is assured, underpins the existence of a diversity of content, including a broad range of opinions, on mainstream channels and on the Internet. The suggestion was made that the National Broadcasters might no longer carry any major sporting events which were currently duplicated on commercial channels, increasing their value to the latter with increased audiences and simultaneously the cost of coverage for the National Broadcasters. But, as was pointed out, viewers to subscription channels would be required to pay for something previously free. Many of the events are celebrated as important elements in the national calendar whose promotion is part of the duties of the National Broadcasters. Diminishing the comprehensive nature of the latter's schedules would also be a step towards the proposition

that the role of the National Broadcasters should be restricted to providing programmes to areas of the output which were commercially
unprofitable.

Several of the interviewees talked at length about the engagement of
the Australian public in broadcasting, citing the consultations which
must accompany the triennial review of the sectors' codes of practice.
As a process, it is inbuilt into Australian broadcasting as a contractual
requirement unlike in the other three countries studied. Against that
must be set the view expressed that the extent of public contact had
been reduced in recent years. One reason suggested for this change was
that ACMA, the latest model of regulatory oversight, did not engage
in public enquiries on the scale of its predecessor. This suggestion has
to be balanced by the belief that the public will not be greatly exercised about broadcasting issues other than those which concerned them
personally, became the subject of parliamentary controversy or were
sensationalised as the scandal over *Big Brother* had been, despite the fact
that the incident had appeared only on the Internet.

India

A brief history

As early as 1927 there was correspondence between Lord Reith of the
BBC and Eric Dunstan, recruited following a career in the BBC to run
the privately-owned Indian Broadcasting Corporation (IBC).[3] The IBC
broadcast in the two main urban areas of Mumbai (then Bombay) and
Kolkata (then Calcutta).

The correspondence shows how Dunstan struggled with both governance difficulties (he encountered resistance from the Board to his ideas)
and lack of resources. These led to his resignation and a government
takeover of the IBC transmitters in 1930. They were operated under
the name of the Indian Broadcasting Service until 1936 when the radio
broadcaster was renamed All India Radio (AIR) and in 1957 was given
an Indian name, 'Akashwani'.

Experimental telecasting began in Delhi in 1969 and a fully fledged
television service, still restricted to Delhi, did not begin until 1965.
Mumbai was added in 1972. Doordarshan, the national television broadcaster, came into being in 1976 and, with AIR, is governed by Prasar
Bharati, the statutory autonomous body that came into being in 1997.

The influence of broadcasting was recognised early on. Dunstan in
1928 talked of the 'public service' that he sought to bring to Mumbai

and the value of (radio) broadcasting 'as a factor of social and industrial stability' for India.

The continuing importance of broadcasting, and the belief within the public service broadcaster that it remains their duty to serve the public interest through their output, is clear in the following comment by Ashok Jailkhani, Deputy Director-General of Programmes at Doordarshan, who talks of the broadcaster as being 'a catalyst for social change':

Interviewer: What you mean by catalyst for social change?

Jailkhani: Catalyst for social change means India being a developing country, India now and what it was 40 years ago, (there is such a) big change. Initially when we became independent , we had very major concerns such as poverty, we had concerns about our (ability to provide sufficient) agricultural produce; we had concerns about so many things. When the green revolution came (and India became self-sufficient in food), the government media had a big role to play, that is what we call catalyst for change. We created awareness, we gave technology, we informed people. So we became a big tool for that change. Similarly there are other issues because in India a large section of the population is still illiterate, so it's only through television or radio that you can reach across the country. From social values to economic values to having a better scientific mind, to creating general awareness. That is what we call catalyst for social change.

Research in the BBC Archives shows that it was the British government which sought to exploit the power of broadcasting to meet its own ends in India. In this extract, the need to use radio broadcasting to maintain a homogenous India serving the needs and interests of the Empire are argued for. Note that, even then, commentators were concerned about the 'Americanisation' of content.

Broadcasting could, and should be the master unifying element if controlled from the centre. There is not only the danger, there is certainly that, in the absence of such unifying forces, systems of education, police, local self-government, and other vital departments of the administration, which are all Provincial subjects, will diverge widely from province to province, with disastrous results to the prospect of creating a homogenous Indian nation ... It would, therefore, be nothing less than a disaster if the threatened Americanisation of Broadcasting in India were allowed to develop, and we were to find, a few years hence, scores of independent broadcasting stations operating in the British Provinces in the Indian States... The control of Broadcasting policy and legislation in India must be kept securely in the hands of the nation government.

(Broadcasting in India, note by Professor Coatman, London School of Economics, 28 July 1934)

Sir Mark Tully, former BBC Correspondent in India, pointed to the restrictive nature of current broadcasting policy in India – and the control by the government – and noted that this was a system openly adopted by the British. However, he argued that future technologies will ensure that the levels of control that the government seeks to impose on broadcasting will not be viable:

The whole development of radio in this country has been hamstrung and the ridiculous thing is India – which justifiably has a longer history of democracy than any other in this region – is the least democratic in broadcasting policy. Particularly with regard to radio. My own suspicion is that they would never have relaxed their control on television but they had to, they couldn't stop the technology. The same technology doesn't yet, but will soon, exist for radio. And then people will start doing radio off shore and we won't be able to stop it.

The importance of the public service broadcasters as the main source of information and content for the larger, rural population remains. AIR now provides coverage to over 97 percent of the population and reaches 90 percent of the total geographic area. The network has a number of national and regional channels, as well as a variety of other stations.

Doordarshan reaches almost 90 percent of the total population through a network of over 1,250 terrestrial transmitters. It has 30 channels – 7 national channels, 11 regional language satellite channels and 11 state network channels. It has recently launched a channel dedicated to the Indian communities scattered throughout the world (DD India), also streamed live on its website. Doordarshan also operates a free-to-air direct-to-home (DTH) service.

Liberalisation of the television market followed in the early 1990s and the Indian Broadcasting Foundation was set up as an industry body for private broadcasters in 1999. In 2007 it was estimated that the total number of cable and satellite homes were in excess of 71.5 million, that is 64 percent of all television homes.[4] Over 200 television channels were operating in 2007 with more awaiting approval. These include a number of language-specific channels. The ownership of the channels is spread over many different organisations and limits are set by the government on levels of foreign investment.

More recently (in 2007) the News Broadcaster's Association (NBA) has been created by the private news channels to address the particular issues of their industry. This is partly in response to the government's attempts to set up a broadcasting regulator (discussed below).

Across this history must be overlaid the particular concerns and cultural interests of India and Indian society. At the time of the interviews, there was a vigorous debate about the conduct of many of the private broadcasters operating in the urban areas. Some of the interviewees reported a concern among politicians and social commentators about the 'Westernisation' of the young (rather than Americanisation, which obsesses many in Europe) through the programming they are exposed to. National security concerns also remain important. As Rakesh Kacker, former Adviser to the Telecommunications Regulatory Authority of India (TRAI) put it,

> Public interest must include national interest. Basically I would say it is two broad categories. One is relating to obscenity, violence, that this might lead to a wrong set of values among, especially, the younger section of the population, and across the different [political] parties, they have the same concern. They feel that television has brought in excessive doses of Western culture, sexuality, violence. So that's one part of it and the other is national interest, which is essentially security.

The concern for national security is significant and a proposed Bill, now lapsed, to cover broadcasting matters allowed the government to take over broadcasting in the event of an emergency:

> In the event of war or a natural calamity of national magnitude, the Central Government may, in public interest, take over the control and management of any of the broadcasting services or any facility connected therewith, suspend its operation or entrust the public service broadcaster to manage it, in the manner directed by the Government for such period as it deems fit.[5]

Alongside this concern is the firm view held by all the interviewees in India that India is proud to be the largest democracy in the world and considers that it is, generally, a tolerant society and that freedom of expression remains an absolute tenet.

India has demonstrated by and large and on a consistent basis, flexibility. There is no part in this country where people belonging to different faiths, speaking different languages, wearing different costumes, eating different cuisines have not been able to live happily. There have been aberrations off and on. But that is temporary and it is no more than an aberration. India has always celebrated consensus building... This country is an old country, an old civilization, but there has always been this open-minded approach to issues, to beliefs, and debate, discussions, contrary views have also been respected. People listen to a contrary view, it's fine. As a matter of fact a basic school of philosophy in India is how to make contrariness exist and so reach the truth.

(Baljit Singh Lalli, CEO, Prasar Bharati)

Legislation

The Prasar Bharati (Broadcasting Corporation of India) Act, 1990

The Prasar Bharati Act, 1990, was passed to provide for the establishment of a Broadcasting Corporation for India. It states that it shall be the primary duty of the Corporation to organise and conduct public broadcasting services to inform, educate and entertain the public and to ensure a balanced development of broadcasting on radio and television.[6] This Act was reviewed in 2000 and recommendations made, but so far only some have been acted upon.

The Cable Television Networks (regulation) Ordinance Act/Network Rules 1994

This Act sets out the rules for cable companies and the programme code that they must observe (along with the advertising code).

The Cable Television Networks (regulation) Act, 1995

This Bill regulates the operation of cable television networks in the entire country so as to bring about uniformity in their operation.

The Broadcasting Services Regulation Bill, 2006 (pending)

In 1997 there was an attempt to pass a Broadcasting Bill that would establish a regulatory authority for broadcasting. This Bill lapsed. There is a Bill still under discussion (in 2008) which seeks to regulate broadcasting services offering entertainment and news services.[7] The preamble to the draft Bill states, '*Airwaves are public property and it is felt necessary to regulate the use of such airwaves in national and public interest, particularly with a view to ensuring proper dissemination of content and in the widest possible manner.*'

The Bill provides for the establishment of an independent authority to be known as the Broadcast Regulatory Authority of India (BRAI). Its purpose will be to regulate and facilitate the development of broadcasting services in India and to incorporate the provisions of the existing Cable Television Networks Regulation Act, which would be repealed. It is this Authority and the draft broadcasting code being considered that have been strongly objected to by industry. In 2008, the Ministry of Information and Broadcasting (MIB) have accepted, in the interim, self-regulatory guidelines to be adopted by the industry. These set out content-related principles and place the responsibility for compliance on the broadcaster.[8]

Licensing

Presently there are no systems for licensing in India apart from those that apply to cable television under the Cable Television Networks (Regulation) Act, 1995. Registration, or licensing, is obtained by applying to the registering authority, currently the Head Postmaster at a Head Post Office of the area within whose territorial jurisdiction the office of the cable operator is situated, along with the requisite fee of 50 rupees. Once registered as a cable operator, the registration period lasts for 12 months and is renewable. All operators must abide by and adhere to the Programme Code as set out in the Cable Network Rules of 1994.

In the proposed Broadcasting Services Regulation Bill, licences would be administered by the Central Government through Licensing Authorities. As before, it would be illegal to broadcast without a licence. Those operating without a licence would be subject to imprisonment and large fines.

Organisational structures

Some observers, Mark Tully among them, felt that those within broadcasting organisations were strongly influenced by outside forces, even though they might try to resist:

> Broadcasting in India is either badly skewed in terms of commercial interests or in terms of government. I suppose I think the public interest is badly served by broadcasting in India and I think it is sad that

attempts to make the government organisations more in the public interest (have) not been very successful.

In fact he thought that the newer media systems (such as content delivered via the Internet) might serve the public better because they were not so dependent on either commercial or government pressures. However, he admitted that it would lead to other difficulties, such as verifying the accuracy or validity of information (issues addressed in the previous chapter on the public interest).

> It's going to be very difficult for the government to control the new media insofar as the new media can lead to the flowering of lots of tiny little independent pathways and blogs, yes it could serve the public better. But my own feeling is that the new media have a huge problem and that is authenticity or reliability or credibility.

Government oversight

The Ministry of Information and Broadcasting (MIB) oversees matters to do with broadcasting and other forms of content, including regulation. It is the MIB which is seeking to drive through the formation of a broadcasting regulator and had facilitated the committee which drafted the Programme Code, currently being disputed.

The TRAI is in charge of developing the commercial aspects of the telecommunications industry, including the development of broadband and other modes of distribution that affect the content industry. While the TRAI makes recommendations and has powers to license and allocate spectrum, it is the government that rubber-stamps decisions. In 2006 the TRAI proposed that regulation of delivery platforms should be regulated by one converged body, but it advised that content issues should be regulated separately.

> The argument being, and I was associated with developing those recommendations, that the kind of intellectual input that you require for content regulation is very different from carriage. For content regulation you require some sensibility about society's tastes and differences, artists who understand these issues whereas carriage, it tends to be about technology, and economics and that kind of thing. The two functions are totally different and they require totally different intellectual inputs. So it was felt that the two should be separate. Unlike the Convergence Bill of 2001, what TRAI had proposed was

that there should be one content regulator across telecommunications, broadcasting and the whole space. And one carriage regulator and even the carriage regulator should do only what TRAI is doing today. On issues such as licensing and spectrum, TRAI would make recommendations but the final authority would remain with the government.

(Rakesh Kacker, former Adviser to TRAI)

This was at odds with a proposed Convergence Bill in 2001, which never got off the ground and which Rakesh Kacker said was unrealistic because the government would not cede that level of control in such an important area.

The government is reluctant to give up its powers in favour of an independent regulator so we thought it would not be realistic to expect an all-powerful regulator to be created and government to be divested of all its powers.

National institutions
Prasar Bharati

(1) *Functions*: As described already, Prasar Bharati is the body that oversees the two national public service broadcasters, Doordarshan and AIR. Its objective, according to the 1990 Act, is

the unity and integrity of the country and the values enshrined in the Constitution; safeguarding the citizen's right to be informed freely, truthfully and objectively on all matters of public interest, national or international, and presenting a fair and balanced flow of information including contrasting views without advocating any opinion or ideology of its own.

The CEO Baljit Singh Lalli described its role thus:

Basically the idea is that a public broadcaster has, would have to take care of, morality in our society , democratic values, secularism and then to promote the cultural diversity at the same time, the oneness of the country. Then economic and developmental issues, governance issues. Basically to improve the levels of awareness of our skills and to ensure that there is some kind of healthy concourse between the policy makers and implementers of the public policy and those for whom the public policy is made, so we provide a forum through our programmes, Doordarshan as well as AIR.

A committee set up to review the Act and to report on the need for Prasar Bharati concluded, in 2000, that

i. Public-service broadcasting is essential in India, and must be seen as a right of all citizens. It must provide a platform for free discourse and debate, while its content must empower people. In the present context, it is essential to have Prasar Bharati in the role of a public-service broadcaster in India.
ii. Prasar Bharati, and its constituents – Doordarshan and All India Radio AIR – must be autonomous and completely free to make their own operational and tactical decisions.

Prasar Bharati has a citizen's charter outlining the public interest commitments of its officers as well its provision for society at large.[9] It was felt by Ashok Jailkhani that the two forms of broadcasting (radio and television), while different, and possibly serving different audiences, were essentially similar in their commitment to a public service ethos.

Our focus, our focal points of communication are the same, the priorities are the same. Obviously the approach will be different because these are two different media essentially, but because at the Prasar Bharati level, there is synergy so on any major issues, any development issues, information issues, we have a common policy.

(2) *Governance*: Prasar Bharati is governed by a board which is constituted of a Chair, an Executive Member, a Finance Member, a Personnel Member, six part-time members, an ex officio Director-General (Akashvani), an ex officio Director-General (Doordarshan), one representative of the Union of the Ministry of Information and Broadcasting, to be nominated by that Ministry, and two representatives of the employees of the Corporation, one to be elected by the engineering staff from amongst themselves and the other to be elected by the remaining employees from amongst themselves. All terms are six years and, in most cases, are served on a part-time basis.

With the exception of the ex officio members, all Board members are appointed by the President of India on the recommendation of a committee consisting of the Chair of the Council of States, who shall be the

Chair of the Committee, the Chair of the Press Council of India and one further nominee of the President of India.

There are no specific criteria in relation to particular political or minority quotas for appointments, but the Prasar Bharati Act states that

> The Chair and the part-time members shall be persons of eminence in public life; the Executive Member shall be a person having special knowledge or practical experience in respect of much matters as administration, management, broadcasting, education, literature, culture, arts, music, dramatics or journalism; the Member (Finance) shall be a person having special knowledge or practical experience in respect of financial matters and the Member (Personnel) shall be a person having special knowledge or practical experience in respect of personnel management and administration.

All recent appointees as CEO of Prasar Bharati have been civil servants. In turn the Prasar Bharati Board appoints the CEO of both the television and the radio broadcasting arms. Other appointments are made internally.

Baljit Singh Lalli did not recognise any problem in being seen as the vehicle for conveying social policy and political messages:

> I don't think there is much interference (from the government). There are issues which we have about making ourselves more free but primarily it will come to funding. If funding is taken care of, (independence) will follow automatically. In any case I have always believed in not being at an arm's length from the government to be a public service broadcaster. I think the government continues to be the greatest repository of public service. So between us and the government I see the possibilities of a great creative partnership.

The President of India has the power to remove members from the Board should they be found guilty of 'misbehaviour' by the Supreme Court, 'moral turpitude', become mentally ill or engage in financial duties outside of their office or cease to live in India.

The Central Government has the discretion of issuing directions to the Corporation as it may think

> necessary in the interests of the sovereignty, unity and integrity of India or the security of the state or preservation of public order

requiring it not to make a broadcast on any matter of public importance specified in the direction.

If the Board fails to carry out the above requirement or does not supply information that the government requires from time to time, then the government has the power to bring it before Parliament and remove the Board members. A parliamentary committee of 22 MPs, voted for by their peers, is established to ensure the Corporation carries out its public service remit as detailed in Section 12 of the Act. In addition, it must prepare an annual report for both Houses of Parliament.

Prasar Bharati is monitored by a Broadcasting Council that ensures it follows its objectives and deals with complaints from outside the organisation. The Council has a President and ten other members, all of whom are appointed by the President of India. In addition, two MPs are nominated to the Council by the Speaker of the House of the People, and two MPs from the Council of States are nominated by its Chair. The President of the Broadcasting Council is a full-time appointment while the Council members are part-time. The period of office is three years. The Broadcasting Council also has the ability to constitute Regional Councils.

At the time of the research for this project, Prasar Bharati was trying to move the two National Broadcasters (radio and television) from government-funded organisations to more autonomous organisations.

(3) *Code of practice*: Prasar Bharati has codes applicable to the two broadcasters it oversees. These cover a variety of areas including the types of advertising that may be carried.

(4) *Funding*: The funding of Prasar Bharati and the two broadcasting organisations was in a state of flux at the time of the interviews. Prasar Bharati had been trying to move to a situation where the government allocates it a budget on a per annum basis to one in which it has a guaranteed source of income. A licence-fee system was provided for in the legislation many years ago, but has never been enacted. This makes forward planning difficult, although Baljit Singh Lalli, the CEO, is determined to try and change this:

> I as a public broadcaster would like to be completely assured of adequate funds. That complete assurance is not there as of now. Government of course gives us fairly large funds. My sense of the issue

is that we should have a system like you have in United Kingdom. Sort of put in place on a regular basis without yearly grants coming to you every now and then. An assured sum, you know that this is your right, like the licence-fee that you have.

The time of interviewing was a time of transition as the public service broadcasters tried to move from organisations that had been part of the government structure to more autonomous bodies, as described by Ashok Jailkhani:

Unfortunately though [Doordarshan is] a corporation, still we have a government kind of audit – it is not even a commercial audit. So it is very difficult for us to face the auditor because the government audit has a different state of mind, a different set of things. Commercial audit is a different kind. So the future of the corporation, the future of the employees, the financial viabilities in the long run, the future competition with public broadcasting on satellite channels. How viable will it be and in what form?...Seeing the television scenario now, there are so many channels, there's so much competition for revenue earnings. Prasar Bharati itself has to decide what kind of staff it would like to have, what should the administrative structure be? Now things have changed with multi-casting. So many things are involved.

The two broadcasters operating under Prasar Bharati receive a grant from that body which covers salaries and other administrative costs, but programme content is paid for primarily through advertising, sponsorship and sales. This is a situation that Baljit Singh Lalli would like to change, at the very least, to lessen the dependency on commercial funds:

Quite frankly...I am not for commercial activities, I want to be a public service broadcaster but I have said on more than one occasion, it is not feasible in Indian circumstances to be a classical, pure public service broadcaster. Let me at least be a substantial one.

Doordarshan

Doordarshan broadcasts to 90 percent of the population. It too has a citizen's charter, serving the public interest and commits to a variety of principles similar to the ones outlined for Prasar Bharati.[10] It pledges to

1. inform freely, truthfully and objectively the citizens of India on all matters of public interest, national and international;
2. provide adequate coverage to the diverse cultures and languages of the various region of the country through appropriate programmes in the regional languages/dialects;
3. provide adequate coverage to sports and games;
4. cater to the special needs of the youth;
5. promote social justice, national consciousness, national integration, communal harmony and the upliftment of women;
6. pay special attention to the fields of education, spread of literacy, agriculture, rural development, environment, health and family welfare and science and technology;
7. provide a comprehensive TV coverage through the use of appropriate technology;
8. undertake at regular intervals auditions for classical dance forms;
9. ensure that the programmes telecast on its channels are in full compliance with the AIR/Doordarshan programme and advertisement code;
10. place basic data about its network, acts and guidelines, list of commissioned/sponsored programmes, defaulting agencies and tender notices in the public domain through its website www. ddindia.gov.in.

What is clear is the two National Broadcasters see their special role as serving citizens throughout India. The distinction is important as the private broadcasters are concentrated around the affluent urban areas. Ashok Jailkhani underlines this:

> India is predominantly an agricultural country, the majority of the population still live in villages. You will hardly see any programme on any (private) channel which addresses the rural audience. You will never see a programme based on agriculture. We have such a huge population, whose economy is run on agriculture. No question of awareness, no question of imparting knowledge to them. Issues of health, empowerment, entertainment for the not-so-privileged sections of society are big issues of concern for us. You will hardly see any programme on education, formal education [on private channels]. You know people in villages and small towns don't have access to specialists, don't have access to good teachers. We do these types of programmes on a regular basis so that when they are watching television they get access to the best programmes. So our programming output is totally different.

All India Radio

All India Radio reaches 97 percent of the population and broadcasts news, music and spoken work programmes, which are the three major pillars of AIR's programming.[11] Programmes for rural listeners are broadcast from almost all AIR stations in different languages and also in local dialects. Special programmes for women are broadcast, and although these programmes provide items of information and of an educational nature, they are also meant to provide entertainment. Organisations such as the BBC World Service Trust work with AIR to provide programming.

Programmes for children and educational programmes cover a wide spectrum: primary, secondary, tertiary and university levels. Programmes aimed at teachers are also broadcast.

Other institutions

Cable companies

Cable companies are also subject to intervention by the government under the Cable Regulation Act of 1995 if it senses that the public interest is being undermined. This can include prohibiting a cable operator from broadcasting. There is also a requirement for operators to broadcast at least two Doordarshan channels.

The proposed Broadcasting Service Regulation Bill includes an additional requirement that the cable networks carry the channels from the two Houses of Parliament, Lok Sabha and Rajya Sabha, as well as having to broadcast a regional language channel.

However, the Managing Trustee of the Public Service Broadcasting Trust (PSBT), Rajiv Mehrotra, is concerned about the financial power of the commercial industry and warns against the government not acting to protect public service broadcasting:

> I also believe that industry works very hard and proactively to stifle Doordarshan and to make sure that Doordarshan does not take off and [the private broadcasters] use their influence and lobby to buy off whatever talent, anybody who is there. And the government simply doesn't simply have the drive, the sophistication, the motivation and the manpower to stand up and take on private industry and private channels. If they did, then it would be very easy because the private industry would capture the top 15%–20% and these guys would then sweep (the rest of the population) far more successfully than they are currently doing by default.

Accountability

India has adopted a Right to Information Act and this has created an environment of greater accountability, as argued by Ashok Jailkhani. With it comes an acknowledgement that one is answerable for the actions of the broadcaster in a way that was not always so rigorous:

> The country has adopted a Right to Information Act very recently, so any person can approach any department – that includes broadcasting – and say 'I want this information'. Anything. You can't escape it, so what I'm trying to say is we're transparent, we're answerable. We were doing this anyway because this medium belongs to the people of India. We have to let them speak, we have to take them seriously, whatever it is. We can't just dismiss them. Now with this Right to Information Act, it has become more stringent.

In the commercial sector, the CEO of NDTV, Narayan Rao, insisted that he is able to keep editorial decision-making separate from any other influence:

> Doordarshan is not independent of government and is not independent of revenue considerations. But we are. Because there is a huge Chinese wall between the editorial and the commercial. We see to that. Part of my responsibility as group CEO is to ensure that. So I have a separate company – NDTV Ltd for example - which does adsales and so on. And I sit between them and the managing editors to ensure that there is no dilution of editorial principles in the interests of commercial considerations.

Engaging with the public

It was clear from the interviews that the public service broadcasters take pride in the fact that their coverage of India and of its population is almost universal. A complex system of state and regional and very local stations was important for those interviewed who saw it as part of their remit to keep local languages, dialects and culture alive. For Baljit Singh Lalli public engagement went far beyond the complaints process or audience measurement systems to the audience itself:

> We have our presence in several parts of the country. Sometimes this goes even beyond the District Headquarters, which represents the very rural hinterland. It's not only broadcast (equipment), our people are physically present there, our transmitters, our studios, our

centres, production facilities are available there. And then regional centres and mobile vans are available. So the voices of the people from below, from where there is no reach, the voices are captured.

The interviews did suggest that consumer bodies and advocacy groups were important in the decision-making process within broadcasting. The MIB had created a committee of people to advise on the drafting of the broadcasting code, for example, although this was decried by the industry as not including enough 'professionals'.

Arvind Kumar, Director (BP&L) at the MIB, talked about other ways in which the public were becoming involved with broadcasting and related issues:

> Various consumers are getting organised through various forums. There are various associations which are coming up. And they have become very vocal now. They are now trying to put pressure on broadcasters either through the media or by demanding that the government lays down suitable policies to create an environment to address their needs.... There have been many changes. Now there is the Consumers Protection Act, also empowering the consumers. And the Right to Information Act.

It is this sort of pressure, Arvind Kumar argues, that makes both government and the industry listen to public voices because

> Ultimately a broadcaster produces what he is able to sell. If he knows that public wants obscenity, then he will produce obscenity. If he knows that there are certain other things to be addressed and there is the audience for it, there is demand for it, and he can find certain advertisers for that programme, then obviously he would like to produce that kind of content.

An influential body is the PSBT, which makes documentary programmes. Rajiv Mehrotra, its Managing Trustee, does not agree that the voices of non-industry players and those interested in PSB are heard by the MIB. His contention is that modern-day broadcasting, and the policy-making for it, are driven by the concerns of industry which in turn serve a relatively narrow population within India, the affluent:

> I think the great challenge that the agendas of public broadcasting face in India is that there is real organised advocacy for its agendas.

And as in most things, it is the ability of the industry to enforce decisions because of their vast resources. There is no consideration for public broadcasting whatsoever, in dialogues and discussions except to the degree that some of us as individuals try and argue to put back the public in public broadcasting – in particular the marginalised and the disenfranchised. Without this India's democracy is undermined. Broadcasting tends to be geared to the elites and more so in India because the divide between the haves and have nots is very large. Naturally, commercially driven television is not interested in people who don't have, who aren't consumers of, the goods and services that advertisers on private channels wish to reach. So that part of India is in effect excluded from the discourse necessary for national democratic decision making. There isn't enough understanding or recognition of the significance or value of public broadcasting; it is usually confused with development support communication.

Those interviewed from the commercial channels, on the contrary, said they did interact with their audiences – Sagarika Ghose, a newscaster at CNN-IBN, used blogs to develop her programmes, to see where the arguments lay:

I want to know what people are thinking. I want to know what they are reacting to, what the issues are. That's why I write my blog. And what is educating to me is people's comments because I read them very carefully. And the comments will often be used in our programme making, we use them as a gauge for opinion because there is no other way of knowing.

Sunil Lulla, then at Times Now (also a private news channel), explained,

We have enough things that we do on the air which ask for citizens' opinions, ask them to send us reports, ask them to write to us, email us, send us a video, dial into us, talk to them on the street, there is enough so-called 'consumer interest interface'. I wouldn't call it activism but interface.

Engaging with the public: Complaints

As in the other territories that have been examined for this project, a complainant is encouraged to write first to the broadcaster. Information outlining the complaints and grievance processes are now made available on air and also on the websites of broadcasters. There are also on-air programmes operated by most organisations which allow for questions (or general complaints) and responses to be aired.

In the commercial sector, complaints go to the broadcaster or they may go directly to MIB. All the news organisations interviewed for this project had structures in place to address complaints, although some felt that the efficacy of their systems was not recognised by the regulators:

> People do write to us, people send us legal notices, they take us to court, all kinds of things happen. . . . If they write to us we respond to them. If they take us to court we happily go and fight if we are right. If we have made a mistake we apologise. We have not had reason to do so to date. Have people taken us to court? Yes, but we have had no reason to apologise to anybody. People can complain to the MIB. When they [MIB] get a complaint they send a notice saying show us why we should not confiscate your licence. The complaint could be anything – it could be someone did not like the colour of what you showed. So it is harsh. There is no genuine redress system. You have got to write to them, they send you notices and sometimes they go ballistic and you have to carry scrolls apologising so the MIB tends to treat the news industry like kindergarten.
>
> (Sunil Lulla, CEO, Times Now)

With regard to Prasar Bharati, and its two public service broadcasters, complaints can be made to the Broadcasting Council, which can

> Receive and consider complaints from . . . any person or group of persons alleging that a certain programme or broadcast or the functioning of the Corporation in specific cases or in general is not in accordance with the objectives for which the Corporation is established.

The Broadcasting Council has complete discretion over how it deals with complaints. The action taken in the case of complaints is not set out but the Council states that it can advise the Executive Member (of the Board) to take *'appropriate action'*. If the Executive Member cannot accept the complaint, then he/she must place it before the Board. The Council can force the network to broadcast matters arising from complaints, where appropriate, in *'such manner as the Council deem fit'*.

With regard to the Right to Information Act there is a complex structure where the complainant can go to the Central Information

Commission. This Commission has the power to summon the CEO of the public service broadcasting organisation (Doordarshan or AIR) to meet with the complainant.

The future

Regulation

It is important to note that, in India, the debate is around broadcasting services and is not yet concerned with the newer media technologies although these are much in evidence, certainly within affluent urban areas. Also all the broadcasters, including the public service broadcasters, have moved or are moving into digital broadcasting and the other opportunities that may be so afforded.

The first, and most heated, debate is around regulation and the attempts by the government, through the MIB, to create an independent broadcasting regulator, the BRAI, and a generic broadcasting code.

As already noted, the public service broadcasters are regulated through the Prasar Bharati Board and, ultimately, by MIB. They have their own codes. The commercial broadcasters are independent bodies and the broadcasting regulator, if created, would regulate that industry. Its function would be to advise government in matters relating to the development of broadcasting technology and any other matters relating to the broadcasting industry. It is proposed that the BRAI will have extensive powers over those who breach licences and stringent penalties enforced on those responsible.

It is envisaged that the proposed BRAI would have one full-time Chair and six full-time members, recruited by a government-based committee. This is opposed by the industry on a variety of grounds; the chief being the perceived lack of autonomy and political independence of the proposed regulator. Industry and others argue there should be a governing body: independent of government, the industry and other groups. Sunil Lulla explained,

For the last ten years the government of India has been trying to create a Broadcast Bill. May it rest in peace. And now recently they have tried to create a broadcasting code. So what the government is trying to do is create a broadcasting regulatory authority and give them some enabling provisions. We believe the BRAI should first be enabled; it should be independent, it should be allowed to do what it has to do rather than be born with clothes.

Arvind Kumar admitted that the recruitment of these officials was much debated:

> There have been some concerns expressed by the people, various associations, broadcasters that the way it [the regulatory authority] is proposed that it may not be able to be totally independent. Because the appointment process proposed should be by the Central Government. Therefore, (the industry and others argue) there should be some Central Committee, so that it ensures that the right kind of people come in, not only the people which the government wants to come in, they should be representing a diverse section of the society who are really concerned for the sector. That is the issue which we are trying to address now. How to make it more independent both functionally and financially and the appointments.

The proposed code seeks to set certain public service obligations on these private broadcasters and to establish a basic set of rules that must be applied. The public service obligations are based around airtime minutage (including commercial airtime, not just programming) given to

- public information messages and
- domestically produced content

This is to try to balance the undue advantage that is seen to be given to private broadcasters who can carry any genres of programming that they wish (as long as they obey national laws). Arvind Kumar said,

> The public interest should meet the needs and aspirations of the people. These should be addressed by broadcasting. It should not purely look at the public as consumers or subscribers. The perspective should be that they are citizens; they have their developmental, social, psychological needs which should be addressed. So that is the perspective. That is the role which presently is being performed only by the public service broadcasters. And... as large sections of population are looking at private channels, so (these channels) also should carry this burden of educating people, of making them good citizens, of helping them develop economically, sociologically.

The commercial broadcasters, spoken to in the course of this project, argue that they have their own internal codes of practice or guidelines. The drive to create a statutory code had been motivated in part by the perception of the invasion of privacy – often of politicians who have been entrapped by 'sting' operations – but also by the manner in which news events had been reported. This is especially true of the reporting of images of violence, often in a sectarian setting. Speaking as the public service broadcaster, Ashok Jailkhani argued,

> If it's a small accident (the commercial channels) will keep on hom-ing in on the body, and show the same footage round the clock. So they don't have that sense of restraint. This is why they need some regulation. That is why the government is thinking of bringing in this kind of thing. We [the national public service broadcaster] are already self-regulated. We are answerable to Parliament. We are answerable to people. We are answerable to government. That is not the case with them.

This alleged sensationalising of news events was underlined by Mark Tully:

> You do need some ability to reprimand and if necessary even to dis-cipline broadcasters. Because total rubbish stories are put on the air, lies are openly told on the air and also one of the worst things which happens is this completely gung-ho live coverage of events which can be very very dangerous indeed because the whole thing is sensation-alised and what you are doing basically is you're just pouring oil onto flames.

This view was contested by most of the commercial news broadcasters that were interviewed. They had their own internal guidelines and felt that they were not sensationalising, although they admitted that some other news channels might.

> What has happened is that most of our competitors have chosen to go the tabloid way with a very heavy emphasis on crime and so on and so forth. So we decided that we cannot go down the tabloid route. It's not something that we can do and not something we will do.
>
> (Narayan Rao, CEO, NDTV)

To counter accusations of sensationalising and to set some common standards, the NBA was formed:

> We have been operating as a well-minded group of colleagues who work well but we become a formal registered society (the News Broadcasters Association) in a few days. We will have a code of practice. We believe in self-regulation. All the news channels in India have a code of practice written into their articles of association – what we do, what we don't do and we follow our self-governance. Our governance practice takes into account the history and tradition of journalism in India.... And most news companies come with journalists from a print background. They have a sense and sensibility. There will be some times, some exceptions but they are not the rule.
>
> (Sunil Lulla, Times Now)

At the time of writing the NBA had taken two codes to the MIB for comment. The first 'Code of Ethics and Broadcasting Standards' addressed these issues of concern and makes commitments not to be partial in the selection of news, to maintain objectivity and impartiality in broadcasting and – in relation to the criticism of 'sting' operations – that such undercover operations should 'be the last resort' of news channels to provide a comprehensive report on the news item. Other parts of the code cover other taste and decency issues, such as the depiction of violence. The second code sets out a dispute resolution process, also self-regulatory. The self-regulatory guidelines described earlier reflect the outcome of these initiatives, and those made by other sectors of the broadcast industry.

There is also the need (noted by the Review Committee in 2000) to make Prasar Bharati a more independent, autonomous body, not as dependent on government for financing and better able to plan its future. However, in the course of the interviews, the role of Prasar Bharati as a mouthpiece of the government – depicted as presenting social messages to the widest population in India – remained clear:

> The Prasar Bharati Act – it also expects Prasar Bharati to project the policies of the government, at least to put them in proper perspective. Whatever is being done for the benefit of the people, they should know of it. The private broadcasters do not find much interest in (these issues). So at least there should be some mechanism by which, if the government wants to say something or project something, then there should be somebody (the public service broadcasters) who can put that perspective before the people.
>
> (Arvind Kumar, MIB)

Digitalisation and the future

The public service broadcaster is already offering a digital terrestrial service and a DTH-via-satellite service. The review of Prasar Bharati argued that the organisation needed to

> move quickly to take full advantage of the full potential and the many possibilities of the New Media such as the Net, Interactive TV, DTH, digital terrestrial broadcasting and the whole area of media convergence. Prasar Bharati must be a step ahead of others in the arena of New Media technology and marketing.

But, due to the cost of equipment, full digitalisation of the Indian market will be difficult. Rakesh Kacker does not find this surprising and points to both the UK and the US as having to postpone planned dates for digital switchover:

> Digitalisation is a good thing and it certainly needs to be promoted. The middle class or upper class can afford these things; certainly there is a market out there which needs to be catered to. (Whether) we can switch over to digital mode and switch off analogue? I think that is far far away in India. Considering the fact that our per capita income is much lower than yours, how are people going to afford it? And if you see the results of the introduction of conditional access systems in parts of Delhi, Bombay, Calcutta, introduced on January 1st this year (2007), the penetration of digital boxes has not been more than 30–40 percent. Of course it's only about 5 months but it's in the initial period that you have your maximum penetration. So these are relatively affluent urban areas and even here the penetration has not been 100 percent. DD [Doordarshan], which caters primarily to rural areas, to people who can't afford direct to home or cable TV, I don't think in the near future we're going to see 100 percent digital coverage (of DD) which will enable them to switch off analogue. They'll have to do both for a long time.

Rajiv Mehrotra of the PSBT sees the new media opportunities as liberating and offering new outlets for expression and the flow of information that had been restricted to those able to afford such access. He argues that there should be public access to the media opportunities opened through the Internet, for example.

> We have been pleading for public access, pleading for a certain bandwidth, whether it is satellite, DTH or whether it is cable. A percentage

of bandwidth must be reserved for public access. There must be an independent authority that manages public access. Just like the print media liberated the flow of ideas and now with user-created content dominating spaces, we must have mechanisms for dissemination till the Internet sufficiently penetrates India. We must build this into all our systems and all our mechanisms of distribution. We have come up against a blank wall. Nobody wants to try and understand it; nobody wants to listen, less so respond to this idea. So I see this great contradiction in the celebrating of our democracy, freedom of expression and all the wonderful things that we talk about. Without creating adequate public spaces in the electronic media much of this is compromised. Whenever the issues or question of freedom of expression has come up in the courts they have always supported it unequivocally. Much more needs to be done.

The United Kingdom

A brief history

Marconi brought wireless technology to Britain in the late 1890s. In 1922 the Post Office agreed to the creation, first, of two experimental stations and then to the establishment of the British Broadcasting Company. As in India, the Board was made up of a group of leading wireless manufacturers. From a small beginning with transmissions from the conurbations of London, Manchester and Birmingham, the Company was an almost national medium by 1925.

Managed by John Reith, the British Broadcasting Company became the British Broadcasting Corporation (BBC) in 1927 when it was given its first Royal Charter. Television broadcasting began in 1936 but the service was closed down in 1939 for the duration of the war. The Coronation of Elizabeth the Second in 1953 was a turning point for television with coverage reaching an estimated 22 million viewers.

ITV was launched as an advertising-supported public service broadcaster in 1955 and BBC2 followed almost ten years later in 1964 as a result of the recommendations of the Pilkington Report. In November 1982, Channel 4 began transmissions as a non-profit-making, but commercially funded, public service broadcaster. The Welsh-language television channel Sianel Pedwar Cymru (S4C) began broadcasting in Wales in the same month but a day earlier as a gesture to Welsh national pride. Channel 5 (now Five), which had some public service requirements placed upon it, was launched in 2002.

In 1982, satellite television services were granted licences, but it was not until 1988 that the British Satellite Broadcasting (BSB) consortium was awarded a licence to operate three channels. It had a number of stringent technical standards to meet as part of the requirements for its licence but, before BSB was able to launch, Sky Television launched four channels in 1990, using the traditional PAL system. Later that year Sky Television effectively took over BSB to form BSkyB, marketed as Sky. BSkyB is now the dominant player in the market.

The governance of both the BBC and the commercial broadcasters (television and radio) has seen many changes. The BBC Board of Governors gave way to the BBC Trust in 2007. Commercial television was licensed and regulated first by the ITA and later by the Independent Broadcasting Authority (IBA), which had commercial radio added to its responsibilities in 1972. The Cable Authority (1985–1990) licensed cable franchises. In 1991 the Independent Television Commission (ITC) replaced both the IBA and the Cable Authority. All commercial television (free-to-air, cable and satellite) came under its regulatory oversight. The ITC was itself merged with other regulatory bodies to form Ofcom in 2003.

It was not until 1972 that commercial radio came into being, the BBC having the monopoly of radio broadcasting in the UK until then. The Broadcasting Act, 1990, removed radio from the responsibilities of the IBA and established the Radio Authority as a new regulator. Like the ITC, it was merged into Ofcom in 2003.

The first 50 years of broadcasting in the UK were punctuated by Government Committees of Enquiry, each with an independent Chair who gave their names to the subsequent reports. From the Crawford Committee, which in 1926 recommended the creation of the BBC as a public corporation to the Annan Committee (1977) proposing an Open Broadcasting Authority to run the fourth television channel, these bodies had a varied record in influencing government policy. But the responses which they drew from the broadcasters provided a kind of accountability. Committees of this kind fell out of favour during Mrs Thatcher's time as Prime Minister, victim of her distaste for a deliberative approach to the solution of a problem she regarded mainly in economic terms.

The most significant recent public debate about broadcasting reached its climax in the Hutton Inquiry (2003). Its purpose was to investigate 'the circumstances surrounding the death of Dr Kelly', a man who had been named as the source for information regarding the then government's public handling of the arguments for entering into the Iraq War. The Inquiry was highly critical of the way in which the management of the BBC, including its Board of Governors, had dealt with events following the initial broadcasting of a news report whose veracity was challenged by the government. In his report, Hutton commented,

> The Governors should have recognised more fully than they did that their duty to protect the independence of the BBC was not incompatible with giving proper consideration to whether there was validity in the government's complaints (about the way in which the story was presented), no matter how strongly worded by Mr Campbell [the Prime Minister's then communications adviser], that the allegations against its integrity reported in [the journalist's] broadcasts were unfounded and the Governors failed to give this issue proper consideration.

Legislation

Wireless Telegraphy Act, 1949

The Wireless Telegraphy Act, 1949, provides for the licensing of wireless telegraphy.

The Television Act, 1954

The Television Act, 1954, permitted the creation of the first commercial television network, ITV. Royal Assent was given to the Act on 30 July 1954. The ITA was established to regulate the new commercial services in the interests of 'good taste', and to award franchises to a network of regional commercial companies for fixed terms.

The Broadcasting Act, 1980

The Broadcasting Act, 1980, was repealed by the Broadcasting Act, 1981, though the provisions of the former remained in force. The most significant effect of the Act was to amend the IBA Act, 1973, giving the IBA the power to establish a second television channel. The process led to the creation of Channel 4 in 1982.

The Broadcasting Act, 1981

This amended and consolidated certain provisions contained in previous legislation (the Broadcasting Act, 1980), including the removal of the prohibition on specified people from broadcasting opinions expressed in proceedings of Parliament or local authorities, the extension of the IBA's functions to the provision of programmes for Channel 4 and the establishment of the Broadcasting Complaints Commission (BCC).

The Broadcasting Act, 1984

The Cable and Broadcasting Act, 1984 provided for the establishment of a Cable Authority to appoint, supervise and promote cable services and for the IBA to facilitate Direct Broadcasting by Satellite (DBS) services.

The Broadcasting Act, 1990

The Broadcasting Act, 1990, established a new framework for the regulation of independent television and radio services, and satellite and cable television. The IBA and the Cable Authority were dissolved and replaced by the ITC.

This Act repealed the Broadcasting Act, 1981, the Cable and Broadcasting Act, 1984, and others.

Included in this was a requirement that the BBC, all Channel 3 licensees, the Channel 4 Television Corporation, Sianel Pedwar Cymru (S4C) and the future Channel 5 licensee procure a minimum amount of programming from independent producers.

The Broadcasting Act, 1996

The Broadcasting Act, 1996 made provision for digital terrestrial television broadcasting and contained provisions relating to the award of multiplex licenses. It also provided for the introduction of radio multiplex services and regulated digital terrestrial sound broadcasting. In addition, the Act amended a number of provisions contained in the Broadcasting Act, 1990, relating to the funding of Channel 4 Television Corporation, the funding of S4C and the operation of the Comataidh Craolidgh Gaialig (the Gaelic Broadcasting Committee). The Act also dissolved the Broadcasting Complaints Commission and Broadcasting Standards Council and replaced these with the Broadcasting Standards Commission. The Act contained other provisions relating to the transmission network of the BBC and television coverage of listed events and relaxed some of the previous restrictions on media ownership.

Communications Act, 2003

The Communications Act, 2003, gave the converged telecommunications and broadcasting regulator, Ofcom, its powers.

Licensing

The main licensing authority for the private sector of television and radio broadcasting in the UK is Ofcom.[12] Once a licence has been granted, the broadcaster is subject to the Ofcom Broadcasting Code, which sets out the standards that are expected of their output in areas such as crime, religion, fairness, sponsorship, privacy and protecting the under-18s.[13]

Television

Three types of licence are available from Ofcom for television broadcasters:

1. Television Licensable Content Service (TLCS) for cable and satellite services.[14]
2. Digital Television Programme Service (DTPS) and Digital Television Additional Service (DTAS) for digital terrestrial TV – Free-view services.[15]

If any licensee fails to comply with the conditions set out in the Broadcasting Act or in the codes, Ofcom can impose penalties ranging from warnings and the requirement to broadcast an apology to fines and the shortening or the withdrawal of a licence.

Radio

In addition to regulating television output and licensing television broadcasters, Ofcom is responsible for licensing all non-BBC radio services, of which there are four types:

1. national commercial services
2. local commercial services
3. community services and
4. restricted services.

When a licence is competed for, applicants are required to provide details of the programme service (or services, in the case of digital licences) that they intend to broadcast if their application is successful. In the event that it is, these details are included in the licence. How detailed the description is depends upon the category of licence; but in all cases, it is a requirement that the successful applicant delivers the service(s) that it said it would at the time of application.

On-demand services

At the time of writing the UK had the only European self-regulatory body for the regulation of on-demand services, the Association for Television On Demand (ATVOD).[16] ATVOD was set up with the agreement of the government following the passage of the Communications

Act, 2003, to regulate non-linear services, that is content delivered via a platform which allows the user to select content and view it at any time. ATVOD is led by an independent Chair, has a code of practice which offers guidelines backed by Guidance Notes, and a complaints process.

It is likely that ATVOD or some similar organisation will become a co-regulatory body following the implementation of the European Union's Audio Visual Services Directive (in 2009). This wide-ranging Directive extends and updates the 1989 TV without Frontiers Directive to include non-linear services such as video-on-demand services.

Organisational structures

I think the basis of the way broadcasting operates is clearly the law, both common and statute, which is agreed by us all democratically and I don't think that anyone has an issue with that. Then there is a system partly of law, partly of regulation which ensures that competition is enabled so that existing players cannot choke off new entrants, can't abuse their market dominance in one form or another... if you are putting public money, either directly from the taxpayer or by some other mechanism, in our case the BBC licence-fee, to create a state-funded broadcaster, then it seems to me not unreasonable that you then attach conditions to that broadcaster which govern at least part, if not all, of its output. I think it can be a rational kind of relationship. I don't think that applies in any way to players in the market who aren't in that category of which Sky is obviously an example. And it's a debateable point the extent to which that state funding is itself a good thing in the first place. But it exists, then yes, we do have some right to ask for a social return on our money.
(Martin Le Jeune, former Head of Public Affairs at BSkyB, UK)

Department for Culture, Media and Sport

The Department for Culture, Media and Sport (DCMS) oversees the broadcasting and creative industries in the UK. With the then entitled Department for Trade and Industry (DTI), now the Department for Business, Enterprise & Regulatory Reform (BERR), it established the converged telecommunications and broadcasting regulatory body, Ofcom, following the passage of the Communications Act, 2003.

The DCMS had responsibility for the preparation of the regulatory framework for the BBC, set out in the Royal Charter of 2006 and the accompanying agreement.[17]

Significant are the two new criteria in the Charter and Agreement that enforce the BBC's public interest remit and provide extra public scrutiny.

These are the BBC's Public Purposes and the public value test (described further below).

The Communications Act gave Ofcom certain responsibilities for all broadcasters, but parts of its remit cover only commercial public service broadcasters. Bill Bush, who formerly worked within the Department, suggested that the lines of reporting were not very clear, especially where Channel 4, the non-profit-making commercially funded public service broadcaster was concerned. Unlike either the BBC or ITV, this left the channel very exposed, he argued, and the government did not adequately 'protect' it:

> It's in an odd position. It's publicly owned, it doesn't have to be held to account by shareholders. (But) it's an accountability-flaw, in that the only shareholder, the government, doesn't even try to hold Channel 4 to account, which is weird, wrong, morally and legally. I don't mean that it's against the law, but...I don't know of another environment in which the shareholder says, 'We own all of you, we don't care what you do.' So it's kind of strange. So its capital model is one in which it is wholly protected, but its revenue model is one in which it's wholly exposed to the market. So in that sense it's an anomaly and if you look purely from the point of view of ownership, it should be far more PSB and far more accountable.

Indeed, relationships between the government and the BBC and the government and the regulator, Ofcom, were discussed during the interviews. The series of events that had led to the Hutton Inquiry were thought by many to be closely linked with the way in which the government and the BBC had interacted with one another – not only during a short specified time, but over a period.

Andrew Ramsay of the DCMS, when discussing an historical event concerning a programme about Northern Ireland, banned by the IBA, insisted that the government should be kept at a distance from broadcasters:

> That's getting a bit closer to the idea that somehow the BBC or the IBA [the then regulator for commercial television], should take a government view, isn't it? Which, of course, isn't what the position is at all...The IBA, I'm sure, didn't take the view because it thought the government wanted it to take that view. It would certainly be quite wrong of the IBA or the BBC to do it for that reason.

Michael Grade, Executive Chairman of ITV (and former Chairman of the BBC as the control of the organisation passed from a Board of Governors to the new BBC Trust), however, spoke of the link between government and the regulator and how that relationship had created uncertainty in the industry:

I am pessimistic about Ofcom's willingness under its present regime to stand up to government. There's a case recently where there was a liberalisation of gambling at government level, lots of casinos. Part of the liberalisation was the lifting of restrictions on the advertising of casinos on television. Sensitive area, important area, where public policy and advertising regulation on broadcasting needed to be in sync. and needed to come up with a policy that was responsible but in tune with the government's desire to liberalise that area of the nanny state. A procedure was set up and we worked through the relevant bodies of the gambling sector, trade association, the BACC – that is the commercial television industry body that worries about copy clearance – and Ofcom. And they went and got input from government and a policy was arrived at after eight months of deliberation and discussion. And that policy was implemented. Prime Minister resigned and Gordon Brown takes over and his first act was to go back on the gambling liberalisation. The Secretary of State ... sends for the gambling sector and tells them that unless they agree to the following new restrictions they will not be allowed to advertise at all. Gambling sector folds immediately because they are not men of the world, they are not experienced in these matters. They fold completely and the whole of the Ofcom process has been subverted and undermined. And not a peep, not a peep ... I find that very depressing.

Richard Hooper, former Deputy Chair of Ofcom, argued that Ofcom – and regulators before it – are indeed independent, but do take soundings from government departments:

I believe very strongly that Ofcom and the Radio Authority and many other independent regulators are actually independent regulators. They are set up by Parliament to do jobs and what the Minister's view is or is not is, in one sense, irrelevant. But we live in the real world. Therefore at Ofcom or at the Radio Authority whenever there were major policy issues we made absolutely sure that we consulted the government. The last thing government wants is surprises. They are allowed to surprise us, but we are not allowed to surprise them. So therefore in any consultation about news, conclusions of reports and so on, they clearly should know what is going on and they should have an opportunity to give their views and those views should be taken seriously.

Tim Toulmin, of the Press Complaints Commission in London, argued, on grounds of freedom of expression, for a distancing from government and control by politicians, not accepting the arguments made by others that elected politicians can act as – and should be – the appropriate representatives of the public.

I was going to say that accountability is one thing and actually healthy in order to shine a light on the workings of the PCC and it's acceptable and healthy to have to go before a public body of people and justify your existence and there's nothing wrong in that. But there is something wrong in supervision, however, by a parliamentary group and the whole idea of self-regulation is to keep the regulation of a free press away from the politicians and so, of course, that boundary is very important to respect.

British Broadcasting Corporation

The British Broadcasting Corporation received its Royal Charter and became state owned in 1926, effective from 1927. The Charter is normally reviewed every ten years, with the most recent Charter coming into effect in 2007.[18] The BBC was granted the latest Charter on condition that it serve the public interest by

sustaining citizenship and civil society; promoting education and learning; stimulating creativity and cultural excellence; representing the UK, its nations, regions and communities; bringing the UK to the world and the world to the UK; and, in pursuing its other purposes, helping to deliver to the public the benefit of emerging communications technologies and services, and taking a leading role in the switchover to digital television.

The latest Charter was particularly important for the changes it has made to the governance of the BBC (see below).

Emergency arrangements

With regard to the BBC, as part of its Charter Agreement, any government Minister

(a) may request that the BBC broadcast or otherwise distribute any announcement, and

(b) may, if that Minister has requested that the announcement be broadcast or otherwise distributed on television or by means of an online service, request that the BBC accompany that announcement with a visual image (moving or still) of anything mentioned in the announcement.

Governance

The BBC is governed and overseen by the BBC Trust which is independent of BBC management and external bodies; it is '*the sovereign body of the BBC*'.[19] The Trust was established by the Royal Charter of September 2006 (effective from 1 January 2007) and replaced the former Board of Governors.

Overseeing the BBC's Executive Board, the Trust has 12 trustees who are appointed by the Queen, on advice from the government, including a Chair, a Vice-Chair and a member for each of the four nations of the UK. Trustees serve for a maximum five-year term, after which they may be appointed for a further and final term on completion of their first.

One of the arguments for creating the Trust was to ensure separation of the Trust (as the managing strategic body) from the day-to-day running of the BBC. The Hutton Inquiry – and the circumstances leading to it – suggested that this separation was not clear when the Governors were 'regulating' the organisation. Michael Grade, Chairman of the BBC following the incident that led to the Inquiry, commented on his analysis of what had happened at the BBC at that time:

It was very clear to me from a distance that where the Board of Governors went wrong, and this was symptomatic of the fundamental problems of the Governors of the BBC, was that they believed very honourably that the BBC in the face of an unprecedented attack from a very powerful government, that the BBC's interests in the survival of the BBC depended on the Governors supporting the institution and the Executive at that time. That was a fundamental mistake because the interests of the institution were best served by getting at the truth and keeping a distance from the Executive. (The Governors) felt that they had to defend the institution and they chose to support the management. And, of course, at the end of the day, management's account of what happened rather came unravelled in the Hutton Inquiry... the Governors should have distanced themselves and that was the heart of the governance problem of the BBC. That was it in stark relief.....that was my starting point – that essentially the ultimate authority, the sovereign body of the BBC, has to be seen to be defending the public interest in the BBC and not the institution by default.

Andrew Ramsay, DCMS, agreed that the Board of Governors had been too close to the Executive, but said this was the case well before the events that led to the Hutton Inquiry. He argued that the structure that the BBC had operated under was no longer practicable in a world with strong competition for audiences and for a place in the communications market. Referring to an event in 2006 where the commercial broadcasters had argued that the BBC's rolling news service (News 24) was not sufficiently differentiated from their news services, he said,

> I think it was clear well before Hutton that there was an issue and that the Governors, whatever they really did were too close to the Executive to be able to persuade the wider competition in this case particularly, that they were taking a balanced view as to where the BBC stood in the world. When there was very limited competition and a very profitable market, then it was much easier for the Governors to operate in that world than it is in one full of lots of competitors. Where this appeared most sharply was in the whole business of the BBC's new services. The consequence of the BBC Governors not having the credibility in the new world that they had in the old, was that decisions about new services got pushed more and more to us and as a department we got very involved in the detail of BBC3 and BBC4 [new BBC channels] etc. etc. It wasn't really government's role. So the new system takes that all out and gives it all to the Trust which is where it should rightly be, but on a basis now which we think stands up to scrutiny from the BBC's competitors.

Michael Grade argued that while it was important that the Trust was outside the day-to-day running of the institution, it was also important that it sat within the BBC, in part because of the scale of the public intervention as a result of the licence-fee.

> They are a financial regulator of the BBC, to ensure that the money is spent fairly ... I kept saying how could you have the sovereign body of the BBC which can only act after there has been a problem. The sovereign body of the BBC representing the public interest has to

be inside the BBC in order to ensure outcomes and not simply to be there after the accident has happened. That is not an acceptable way to manage the public's money in this particular case. And that argument held sway.

Andrew Ramsay at the DCMS agreed with this, pointing to pressures from industry and others, at the time of the drafting of the new Charter, to hand over responsibilities for the BBC to a body that sat outside the organisation:

We were always aware that we were creating something which didn't really exist anywhere else. We went for a single BBC solution rather than taking in particular the regulatory stuff out of the BBC and giving it to somebody else, which various people advised as a possibility. In doing this we were aware that the Trustees would have a role which isn't purely regulatory, it's more like the IBA perhaps in some ways, but they were also there to agree the strategy and represent the interests of the licence-fee payers back into the BBC. So it's very much a BBC solution. But we have built into the Charter where the distinctions need to be placed in the relationship between the Executive and the Trust. And from what I see those distinctions are being maintained.

The House of Lords Communications Committee, reporting in August 2007, expressed concern at the supposed distance between the Trust and the Executive Board, arguing that they need to be aligned in their overall objectives as a public service broadcaster:

Article 10 of the new Royal Charter states that there is no longer a formal Chairman of the BBC. 'The Chairman of the Trust may also be known as the Chairman of the BBC. In [the Committee's view], this is an honorary title, as the members of the BBC will never act as a single corporate body, but only as members of the Trust or Board to which they belong'... The fact that the BBC will never 'act as a single corporate body' means that the Chairman and Director-General will no longer stand together representing one organisation (despite the seemingly contradictory statement... that 'the Corporation that is the BBC shall comprise all the members of the BBC Trust and the Executive Board'). This is a radical change and one that concerns us.[20]

Lord Rees Mogg, who had previously been Vice-Chair of the BBC Board of Governors, also questioned this degree of separation between the Executive and the Trust:

> I don't see how making the Board of Governors into a Trust and making them more remote with less feeling that they have direct responsibility is actually going to improve accountability.

Michael Grade stressed that he had brought practitioners onto the Board of Governors and then onto the Board of the Trust. This was an important move as it gave the regulated industry confidence that the regulator understood their challenges:

> First time in the history of the BBC that they actually had practitioners on the Board of Governors and on the Trust. I think that's very helpful, I think it gives the Executive confidence that their problems are being understood by people who have been there and done it.

For Georgina Born of Cambridge University, this confidence - that the Trust would be sufficiently different from the previous Board of Governors because of the sort of people on it - was insufficient reason for confidence about the ability of the Trust to be an effective regulator of the BBC:

> It's not just about having a new kind of person on the Trust, such as industry people. Until you have a different process of appointment to the Trust, which is truly independent and transparent, so that the Trust is really seen to be very different from the Governors in its make-up, I think that its legitimacy is in doubt. It matters hugely that the process of appointment is open, independent of government and seen to be, and therefore results in new kinds of people being on the Trust.

The Trust is supported by a Trust Unit, which provides expert and independent advice to members and it can call on outside experts when necessary. The Executive Board is defined in the Royal Charter as having

> responsibility for delivering the BBC's services in accordance with the priorities set by the Trust and for all aspects of operational management, except that of the Trust's resources.

Remit

The Trust is responsible for *'setting the overall strategic direction of the BBC, including its priorities, and in exercising a general oversight of the work of the Executive Board. The Trust will perform these roles in the public interest, particularly the interest of licence fee payers.'*[21] The Trust also acts as a final office of appeal for the general public in circumstances where the complainant has exhausted the BBC management's complaint procedure. Steven Barnett, of the University of Westminster, describes the Trust's role as fundamentally different from that of the Governors because of its requirement to consider the impact of any BBC service on the UK's communications market:

> I think what the authors of the Bill, the new Charter, would argue is that ... they [the Trust] need to acknowledge that there are two separate constituencies. And that's what's new. The notion of accountability to the licence-payer is absolutely there in black-and-white, four square, but accountability to the commercial sector is something that is brand new and I suspect the authors of the Charter would say that that is a legitimate expanded definition of accountability.

Public Purposes

The 2007 Charter sets out how the BBC can serve the public interest through Public Purposes, described in Chapter 3.[22] Georgina Born of Cambridge University was heartened, as were others interviewed, by the recognition that not all essentially qualitative measures could be quantified. The fact that this had been recognised on the face of the Charter was important.

> In the 2003 Communications Act, when you look at the particular section where it adumbrates the values of the public service system, all kinds of very productive things were stuck in: reflecting the cultural diversity of Britain back to itself and so on. It's not a bad attempt to bring into law a bunch of crucial back-up criteria ... What pleases me, if that is what is going on in these various mechanisms in law and in the Charter, is the recognition that law should indeed be used to back up interpretation and practice in relation to public service broadcasting.

Mark Thompson, Director-General of the BBC, saw the Public Purposes as an extension – or codification – of the way the BBC has always addressed its objectives and its responsibilities. He finds them helpful in the current media environment:

> In the late 1920s, the BBC was thinking quite hard about what information, education, entertainment and so forth might mean. But it's partly because of the flavour of the times that almost everyone in this place likes the idea of as much specificity as possible. And last year's [2006] White Paper is another attempt to be slightly more explicit... the nature of convergence and, in particular, the nature of the way audience, or public, behaviour with media is changing, it seems to make more sense to talk about the provision of a body of content against a Public Purpose. So, for example, news provision against a Public Purpose around the idea of supporting democratic institutions and the national debate.

He continued,

> In a sense what matters most is the body of content and what matters rather less than it used to is precisely how you access that content. people now are accessing news in lots of different ways – Blackberries, Ceefax, Web, continuous news channel – but they might also in a more classic way be watching the news on BBC One. I think the Public Purposes are quite a useful way of actually thinking clearly about this relationship with the public. They give us the money, they get these broad propositions which I think you can cluster reasonably sensibly around different Public Purposes. Not always, by the way, in a completely genre-specific way – it's quite important that we don't think that Public Purposes can only be done by certain genres. It's quite possible to imagine that *Eastenders* [soap opera, popular in the UK] is a rather good vehicle, for example, for promoting public information and education about domestic violence. That might be a better way of doing it in some ways than a documentary about domestic violence which will only be watched by people who know they're interested in it and so on. The reason that you congregate your strategy around the Public Purposes is that it's quite a good way of thinking about the future.

David Levy, at the BBC at the time of interview, agreed that the Public Purposes were a useful way to focus thinking about the organisation's strategies and objectives:

BBC management are now forced to be absolutely crystal clear about what they want to do, why, how does it fit with the purposes the BBC has, what's it going to do in reach and share and all the rest of it and initially that has been a very tough process for people within the BBC but I think it's a good process in terms of making us think hard about what we're focusing our efforts on.

Tony Prosser, Professor of Public Law, Bristol University, however, expressed some concern about the way in which concepts such as those described as the Public Purposes could be quantified and put into a suitable framework for market assessments.

Given that competition concerns have surfaced so much over the last decade, I think it's useful to have someone who is economically literate there [BBC Trust]. The danger, of course, is that you tend to see things through a particular sort of methodology, through a particular set of theories which are not necessarily appropriate when you are dealing with things like social solidarity, if you like, as a purpose of Public Service Broadcasting and regulation.

Public value test

The Royal Charter also provides for a Public Value Test, which means that any significant proposals from BBC management for change in direction or for the setting up of new services must be subject to full and public scrutiny.[23] The BBC Trust uses it to determine the value of such a change to the public and Ofcom undertakes a market impact assessment. If it is suggested that the public value created is greater than the potential negative impact on the market, then the proposal will go forward for consultation. At the end of the consultation, the BBC Trust will decide whether or not to approve the proposal. Nicholas Kroll, Director of the BBC Trust, saw this formal acknowledgement of the duties of the BBC to the wider marketplace and to industry, in particular, as necessary:

There wasn't a sense of confidence in the industry and more widely that the Governors were taking a dispassionate view of various propositions put to them by the Executive. I think at a time of big technological and market change those sorts of issues within the industry were becoming more important, with the market place in particular concerned about the BBC's impact on their business and the sense that the BBC wasn't actually being adequately scrutinised before it was moving into territory which had its impact elsewhere.

Andrew Ramsay explained that the encouragement of a healthy market, in which the BBC is a player, is to the benefit of all licence-fee payers:

> The licence-fee payers have primacy, but it doesn't mean to say that dealing with the interests of other broadcasters and the rest of the industry isn't very important... It's actually in the interests of licence-fee payers that the rest of the market functions and the BBC doesn't prevent that.

Funding

The principal means of funding the BBC is through an annual television licence-fee, required by all households that have a broadcast television set in the UK. The cost of the licence (in early 2008, £135.50 for colour television) is set by government and enforced by criminal law. The revenue is paid into a central government Consolidated Fund and allocated by the DCMS and Treasury. The BBC also has a commercial arm, BBC Worldwide, which derives income from commercial enterprises and overseas sales of its programmes.

There is much debate about the level of public intervention that is required to serve public interest needs. When asked, Michael Grade argued that there needs to be public intervention (as in the licence-fee for the BBC, or reduced charges for spectrum, as in the case of the commercial public service broadcasters) to ensure innovation (as an example) where the market may not be prepared to take a risk.

> The market pushes everything into the narrow mass of new directions and in order to sustain the arts you do need some public intervention. There is a public interest, it seems to me, in the new and high-risk taking and so on that perhaps the market can't deliver and I don't see why broadcasting should be any different. We have chosen in this country to make that intervention essentially through the licence-fee and the BBC. There have been other forms of intervention – the price that was extracted from the commercial television companies in the days of the monopoly. In return for the monopoly which... had ensured public service competition to the BBC, ensured a range of programmes that you wouldn't have got from a purely commercial market-driven system which is what you have in the United States, with PBS.

In correspondence, Steven Barnett questioned whether the Trust is able to balance its two roles.[24] One is to act as the protector of the public interest, holding management to account and protecting the BBC's responsibilities to the licence-fee payer in areas such as the institution's independence versus its other role, holding management to account for decisions that impact on commercial competitors. He argues that the Trust is weighted towards the latter rather than the former and that will create potential conflict in the future:

> The Trust will need a great deal of determination to stand firm in the face of fierce attacks from commercial competitors, backed by large sections of the press who will be seeking to whittle away the BBC's areas of activity and progressively to reduce its reach and influence. The sheer number and weight of forces that will be ranged against it – which in some cases will almost certainly include the powerful regulator Ofcom – will inevitably result in the BBC being denied opportunities to vary, extend, reinterpret or expand services in a manner that over the last 80 years helped to ensure its vitality at the heart of British culture.[25]

Ofcom

Governance

The Ofcom Board can have up to 10 members, including the Chair, appointed by the Secretary of State. Executive appointments are made internally within the organisation. Georgina Born questions whether, in the attempt to get away from criticisms of only 'the great and good' being appointed to such institutions, Ofcom has leant too far on a system of appointment which is unbalanced in terms of skills needed for a converged regulator, covering both content and economic issues.

Remit

Ofcom was established by the Communications Act, 2003, as the independent regulator for the communications industries in the UK. It inherited the duties of five regulatory bodies:

- the Broadcasting Standards Commission
- the Independent Television Commission
- the Office of Telecommunications (Oftel)
- the Radio Authority and
- the Radiocommunications Agency.

Under the Communications Act its statutory duties are as follows:

3(1) It shall be the principal duty of Ofcom, in carrying out their functions;

(a) to further the interests of citizens in relation to communications matters; and

(b) to further the interests of consumers in relevant markets, where appropriate by promoting competition.

Ofcom describes its specific duties as falling into six areas:[26]

1. ensuring the optimal use of the electromagnetic spectrum;
2. ensuring that a wide range of electronic communications services – including high-speed data services – are available throughout the UK;
3. ensuring a wide range of TV and radio services of high quality and wide appeal;
4. maintaining plurality in the provision of broadcasting;
5. applying adequate protection for audiences against offensive or harmful material;
6. applying adequate protection for audiences against unfairness or the infringement of privacy.

The Communications Act set out a three-tier structure for the regulation of broadcasting content:

Tier 1 sets out negative content regulation requirements, through the Broadcasting Code, for *all* broadcasters (such as standards of programme content, protection of children, advertising standards and impartiality);

Tiers 2 and 3 apply *only* to the public service broadcasters, namely the BBC, S4C, Channels 3, 4 and 5, and public teletext and defines their 'individual public service remit':

Tier 2 sets out specific, measurable requirements, for example quotas on independent/original production and regional programming and production, and educational programming.

Tier 3 excludes the BBC and provides for those other areas of public service output where Ofcom cannot set quotas and includes areas such as an obligation to produce an annual statement of programme policy and an annual report of performance.

Ofcom is also the lead competition authority (sharing concurrent powers with the Office of Fair Trading). Steven Barnett talked of the difficulties that Ofcom, as a converged regulator, might have, as it balanced its remit as champion of the consumer and the consequent commercial sector responsibilities – with its public sector responsibilities and its duty to the citizen.

> Those battles will go on within a converged regulator because there are always going to be battles between the commercial sector's demands to go out and make its money and the public interest responsibilities of the regulator saying we need to do the best for the nation, the totality of viewers and listeners. But those tensions, those battles, which have always been implicit in broadcasting (and were) externalised, and are now internalised.

Damian Tambini, Senior Lecturer at the London School of Economics, also pointed to the dilemma that may be encountered by any organisation where the brief spans many areas – the nature of the debate about the objectives of that organisation will differ depending on the environment surrounding the issue. Can one organisation balance all the needs and objectives?

Structures

In addition to the Ofcom Board and the Ofcom Executive, responsible for the running of Ofcom and structured with 'Partners' in charge of particular areas, Ofcom has a number of committees that report to the Board. Those of particular interest to this project are as follows:

1. the Ofcom Content Board: this committee, a subset of the main Board, considers the regulation of television and radio programming. The Chairman of the Content Board is the Deputy Chairman of Ofcom.
2. The Content Sanctions Committee: this Committee oversees sanctions relating to content or content-based cases in broadcasting.
3. The Radio Licensing Committee: this Committee licenses radio broadcasting.
4. The Fairness Committee: this Committee considers fairness and privacy complaints in broadcasting.
5. The Election Committee: this Committee considers disputes about party election broadcasts and the application of impartiality rules.

6. The Audit Committee: this Committee has a Chair, independent of Ofcom, and oversees the auditing process within Ofcom.
7. Ofcom & BBC Joint Steering Group: the Steering Group operates under an Ofcom/BBC Memorandum of Understanding (MOU), and is concerned primarily with the market impact assessments already described.

There is also a Consumer Panel which represents the interests of the consumer in a variety of ways. Peter Lunt, Professor in the School of Social Sciences and Law, Brunel University, reflected on the change this represented as the regulator now had an independent, but linked, body that was part of its overall structure and which brought the knowledge and experiences of people with different needs

> Certainly the way Ofcom has set up the consumer panel, it's based on a very different notion of representation. Firstly it's orientated towards consumers, and secondly towards a very specific vulnerable group. Some of the people who make up the body, or the consumer panels, previously worked in a more diverse set of bodies, either in the industry or civil society, NGOs. Another kind of accountability then is the connection between the regulator, the broadcaster and civil society.

Ofcom's Content Board is part of the main structure of Ofcom. As such it is different from the Consumer Panel, as well as serving very different areas of responsibility. Tim Suter, Partner, Content and Standards, at Ofcom at the time of the interview, was asked whether he thought the relationship of the Content Board to the Main Board had worked well. He answered by suggesting that its function and the outcomes had been rather different than might have been envisaged when it was set up:

> Having two boards is a peculiar structure and it's not that it doesn't work, but it probably doesn't work as people thought it would. When Ofcom was established, people assumed that the reasoning behind the Content Board was that Ofcom needed a board which, focusing solely on content issues, would be able to bring to bear that degree of single-minded expertise and energy that might not be possible if the forum which considered it was also considering telecoms and spectrum issues. People doubted that the Main Board would have the time to do it, especially as content issues have the potential to dominate

the front pages of the red tops in a way it is quite rare to get a spectrum issue to do.... The broad agreement between the two boards is that where content decisions are purely content, they will be taken by the Content Board and where they have a significant economic dimension or where they will have a particular bearing on the health or vitality or the prospects of the sector as a whole, then the Main Board should take the decision on the advice of the Content Board. In practice it is not always straightforward to determine those decisions that are purely content in their remit and don't have such an economic dimension that they should go to the Main Board. If you take something like the setting of quotas for the level of original productions which the public service broadcasters should make, that clearly has a very substantial economic dimension to it, so the decision is going to be made by the Main Board, but on the recommendation of the Content Board. Working that through has taken a little while. It's not impossible, but it takes careful thought.

What Tim Suter thought worked well were the complaints systems whereby decisions on complaints were taken at staff level and recommendations made to the Sanctions Committee about the sort of sanctions that should be applied in the event of a breach of the Broadcasting Code.

Funding

Ofcom is funded by fees paid by companies licensed under the Communications Act, 2003, and also by grants and loans from the government for particular issues.

Licensees

Ofcom licences all commercial radio and broadcasting services. In addition, since 1990, the regional Channel 3 companies (the ITV Network), GMTV, Channel 4, S4C in Wales and Five (formerly Channel 5) must provide public service programming, which is overseen by Ofcom.

ITV (Channel 3 companies) – Quota for news, current affairs, independent and European programming, children's and religious programming, and output containing subtitles, signing and audio description. In addition, Channel 3 stations are legally obliged to screen party election broadcasts on behalf of all the major political parties, and also other political events such as the Budget.

Channel 4 – The public service remit for Channel 4 is the provision of a broad range of high-quality and diverse programming which in particular demonstrates innovation, experiment and creativity in the form and content of programmes; appeals to the tastes and interests of a culturally diverse society; makes a significant contribution to meeting the need for the licensed public service channels to include programmes of an educational nature and other programmes of educative value; and exhibits a distinctive character. The remit also involves an obligation to provide schools programming and a substantial amount of programming produced outside of Greater London.

Five – A commitment as a public service broadcaster to provide programmes in a broad range of genres including current affairs, arts, science, history, religion and children's programmes.

Commercial radio also has public service obligations. However, the requirements imposed for commercial radio are generally fewer, normally demanding only a minimum level of news.

In 2004, Ofcom consulted on its first Public Service Broadcasting Review; the second is underway (in 2008).[27] The first Review established certain purposes and characteristics of PSB:

Purposes

To inform ourselves and others and to increase our understanding of the world through news, information and analysis of current events and ideas

To stimulate our interest in and knowledge of arts, sciences, history and other topics through content that is accessible and can encourage informal learning

To reflect and strengthen our cultural identity through original programming at UK, national and regional level, on occasion bringing audiences together for shared experiences

To make us aware of different cultures and alternative viewpoints through programmes that reflect the lives of other people and other communities both within the UK and elsewhere

Characteristics

High quality – well-funded and well-produced

Original – new UK content rather than repeats or acquisitions

Innovative – breaking new ideas or re-inventing existing approaches, rather than copying old ones

Challenging – making viewers think
Engaging – remaining accessible and attractive to viewers
Widely available – if content is publicly funded, a large majority of citizens need to be given the chance to watch it.

The previous Review had noted that there would be a deficit in the support of PSB as television moves to digital, audiences for terrestrial analogue commercial television continue to decline and the value of analogue licences – which include substantial PSB obligations – therefore continues to diminish.[28]

Complaints

All the broadcasters have their own complaints procedure, as do the on-demand services. However, the regulatory bodies, the BBC Trust, Ofcom and ATVOD also have established complaints systems in place.

BBC

The BBC has a three-stage public complaints procedure. If a complaint is regarding impartiality, inaccuracy and some commercial issues, it must be dealt with by the BBC. Ofcom deals with other issues under the Broadcasting Code. The three stages in the BBC are as follows: -

1. A written response in three days after which, if a mistake has been made, there will be an apology and, if appropriate, an online correction will be published.
2. If the complainant is not satisfied, a further complaint can be made to the Editorial Complaints Unit (ECU).
3. If still not satisfied, then a representation can be made to the BBC Trust's Editorial Standards Committee (ESC).

The BBC publishes online a quarterly report of its complaints in the case of the first stage and ECU complaints. It also publishes details of complaints settled by the ESC on a monthly basis.

Ofcom

When Ofcom receives a complaint it must ask the broadcaster for a copy of the programme, which is examined by the Executive to see if it is in breach of the Broadcasting Code. Ofcom also asks for a response from the broadcaster to the complaint. Considering these, Ofcom will mark the complaint as either upheld or not upheld, or alternatively 'resolved'. Outcomes of complaints are published on the Ofcom website and often broadcast on the relevant channel/radio station concerned. Penalties imposed by Ofcom can include considerable financial fines and the revocation of a broadcaster's licence.

ATVOD

ATVOD will direct the complainant first to the provider of the content that is subject to a complaint. If the matter is not resolved satisfactorily it can be brought back to ATVOD. If ATVOD's decision is not agreed with, the complainant or the service provider can take the matter to the Independent Complaints Adjudicator appointed by ATVOD. Penalties can include financial fines and the revocation of membership.

The Press Complaints Commission

The Press Complaints Commission has a complaints structure which includes a complaints adjudicator and charter commissioner.

Engagement with the public

The earlier chapter on accountability had considered different forms of engagement with the public. Advocacy groups are not as common in the UK as they are in the US and, to a lesser extent, in Australia and India. However, in the UK, research – market and social – is used widely by organisations to understand the way in which the public might think, or what it might require. The transition to the new BBC structure and the work leading to the new Charter were heavily predicated on research, and Ofcom, committed to evidence-based actions, uses public consultations and research widely. David Levy accepted that research has limitations but said it sets a discipline and an 'overarching framework' in which to work.

> I think all of this comes back to the mood of the times, a view that you need to be able to quantify much better to demonstrate the value of what you're delivering in public services more generally, but there are limitations to how far you can go, but that's what we're trying to do and trying to introduce a comprehensive, but simpler overarching framework that applies to everything the BBC does rather than multiple different ones.

Similarly, Helen Normoyle, Director of Research at Ofcom, talked of the need to structure research intelligently, to build it so that it can answer the questions that are being asked:

The first step is really grounded in a good understanding of what the critical project questions are and project issues as I said before. There's a general understanding that, yes, we really need to gather the evidence and do the research, but the first step is having a really, really good understanding of the strategic issues and the strategic questions that are being raised and then from that we would work out, well, what is the evidence base that's required for the project. And then you ask: do we need to talk to industry, do we need to talk to stakeholders? You know, what type of stakeholders? Do we need to talk to consumers? Is this a consumer and/or citizen issue? And that then gets into, takes one further down getting an understanding. Is this something where qualitative approach is more appropriate or do we need a quantitative or do we need a mixture of both? Do we need one where we have a complex set of issues that we need to present to people? You know, does that mean that a citizen jury or a deliberative type approach is going to be more appropriate or is it pretty straight-forward, people will be comfortable with responding and individually in which case it's more of a quantitative type survey. So we have a tight process within the research team for how we work with our colleagues in the other departments, whether it's the Content Board or with the strategy market development group or whatever, to help us work out the nature of the research that we would conduct.

But a couple of interviewees cautioned against the blanket acceptance of research and recognised the need for interpretation of what was being said:

> Very romantic – the idea that if you don't have any editorial process and allow everybody to say (whatever they want)... in some magical way the result will be a reliable result. And it just isn't.
>
> (Lord Rees Mogg)

Talking about the different starting points of researched groups, Peter Lunt said,

> One of the problems there is that there were clearly problems articulating what exactly is public opinion, due to the diversity of different public stances. So that shows quite clearly the difficulties defining public opinion from what is in the interests of the public.

Andrew Ramsay, of the DCMS, also talked about the need to mediate public opinion. Helen Normoyle acknowledged that Ofcom was sometimes accused of consulting too widely and too often. Georgina Born wondered if there was not a superfluity of consultations at times:

> What was noticeable was that, as things hotted up around 2000, as the new digital plans were coming in, there was a rash of competitive public reports and consultations. That's when it seemed to explode: there was report after report after report being produced by the DCMS, by the BBC, by the BBC's rivals: a kind of competitive public report production, if you like.

On the basis of her research on the transformation of the BBC in the 1990s and early 2000s,[29] Georgina Born suggested that all research should not be outward-facing but should take the temperature *within* the major broadcasting and production organisations as well:

> It seems to me that we need a research function [in the BBC] focussed upon those things, which is independent of the Executive and tells you something about what's happened, maybe in hotspots: what is the feeling on the ground about resources. And above all, when lots and lots of cuts to production are being handed down, how is it looking on the ground among the producers and commissioners, how do current policies impact on their capacity to fulfil the remit? These are very, very serious issues. So you need a research function within the organisation and reporting to the Trust that is focused on the organisation itself – a kind of internal, honest, non-spun research mechanism that speaks back to the Executive and analyses how current policies are playing out.

Penny Young, Head of Audiences at the BBC Trust, suggested it might be important to find a new set of terminologies to describe the new way of thinking:

> Interviewer: What we used to call 'hard to reach' with a very BBC flavour?
>
> Young: There is a problem with the term 'hard to reach' because it implies the problem is with the consumer, as if they are being difficult. We tend to talk about 'underserved audiences' and sometimes we talk about the 'seldom heard' – particularly in the context of consultations. All of these labels can be a bit off-putting though. The important thing is that we focus hard on doing better among such audiences.

Georgina Born agreed with this:

> The public is not a statistical aggregate as it's considered to be by
> opinion polling. This relates to long-standing critiques of polling, of
> aggregate models of the public. There is no such totality. It seems
> to me that the public can be conjured up through very good mar-
> ket research, but in answer to particular questions, to gain particular
> insights, and that's where the use of multiple kinds of sophisticated
> market research can be helpful. For example, in researching whether
> and how a public that is supposed to be addressed by a new channel
> is exposed to that channel: this seems to me an entirely appropriate
> and very productive use of audience research – to check whether a
> particular segment of the public that it is intended should be reached
> is actually being addressed. In other words, we should understand the
> public as an aggregate which is called into being at specific junctures
> by particular issues and acts and events.

Future

A previous comment by Michael Grade had suggested that the earlier,
monopolistic, model of broadcasting had allowed greater risk-taking and
innovation in programming. The economist Andrew Graham, Master of
Balliol College, Oxford, agreed that

> The monopoly power meant that it didn't matter if every programme
> didn't maximise its audience – you could take a certain kind of risk
> and the company didn't go bankrupt. It's like…in economics there
> are various models of very cut-throat competition and in those mod-
> els the people can't undertake research and development because it
> doesn't pay and they have to offer the lower prices. Double-glazing
> salesmen are the archetypal kind of contemporary example. As the
> digital channels have opened up, more and more people have come
> in so competition has become more cut-throat and the scope for
> doing these other things – like taking risks or making a programme
> which requires a lot of research – has decreased. People these days
> hate monopoly. But a degree of monopoly which gives you a bit of
> spare capacity is actually rather desirable. It's a very unfashionable
> attitude to defend monopoly, but it has its uses.

Among the UK interviewees, it was concerns such as these – the
risk of a lack of innovation in content production or the loss of
production skills – that were often discussed when the future of

broadcasting was considered. This has been recognised by the government in their document *Creative Britain: New Talents for the New Economy*, which sets out government commitments to encourage the creative sector.[30]

> Thinking about the more important question for me...is making sure that we have in place the training and opportunities for digital new media skills, rather than necessarily for traditional broadcast programming. Now I think that there is a risk, because new media tends to be dominated even more than traditional broadcast programming by the US, that the UK may fall behind, so I would – if you were asking about a public policy intervention which is focused on production training and skills, which I think you were – I suspect the focus there should be new media rather than old.
>
> (Robin Foster, former Partner, Ofcom)

Andrew Ramsay thought that the market would continue to produce high-quality content as there was a demand for it, although he accepted this may not continue for all time.

> If we are just talking about the BBC, it has 10 years' confirmed existence over the new Charter period, supported by the licence-fee. While there is a BBC and there is still some form of linear channel, I believe people will watch it. In multi-channel households, most people continue to watch the public service broadcasters. I think you'll find that will continue. Whether the wider, as we were saying earlier, range of commercial public service broadcasters continues in their current form I think is an open question. There has got to be something in it for them. Whether they do or they don't, I imagine they, like the purely commercial broadcasters, will produce something that is of public service quality. There seems, for the moment, to be a demand for it. I imagine that will continue. Whether in 50 years' time, there will still be a demand for it, I don't know.

Martin Le Jeune, former Head of Public Affairs, BSkyB, echoed the view that the market would demand quality programming as part of its choice of content:

> I have a considerably higher opinion (A) of customer demand, for example. I do not think quality news, documentaries, current affairs,

religious or children's programming are going to die because people are not compelled to provide them. There is a market demand for them and it will continue. (B) I have a much higher opinion than most people seem to have of the contribution made by the multi-channel sector, including Sky, where that market demand is being demonstrated on a day-to-day basis. And if we are not hung up too much... about UK-originated material as opposed to quality material of all kinds, we can see that the doom of public sector broadcasting, the demise of public sector broadcasting has been much exaggerated, I believe.

Nevertheless, the particular role that broadcasting, particularly PSB, plays in the social or cultural fabric of a country was underlined by more than one interviewee. Tony Prosser, Bristol University, said,

If you believe that consumer choice is the only value, you would say that it doesn't matter, that having lots and lots of digital channels and the Internet is fine. But again consumer choice is not the only social value. One of the other important social values is actually learning, developing your preferences, developing understanding and I don't think that's what can be offered in the same way by, say, the Internet. It's incredibly useful for me if I want to find out something about France or Italy or the United States to look up the answer on the Internet or Wikipedia or whatever... It's not a way of getting into a culture and that is what I think public service broadcasting at its best can do. So that's why a highly consumer-controlled approach is not necessarily going to provide the same kind of support for those values. It can support other values: freedom of expression, for example, obviously the Internet is very important for that, though the important thing is that it is not seen as the only way in which you have freedom of expression.

It seemed to Robin Foster that the need to guide people to a variety of material, as part of the knowledge-creation role of the communications sector, would become increasingly important:

I think you still need ways of finding out about new programming and new talent and so the challenge is going to be for the main broadcasters of the future to still have a key role in packaging. Lots of people still go into video stores, DVD stores or record stores and browse around and they are open to suggestions about what they might like. I think finding the broadband equivalent of that is the challenge for broadcasters.

Moving from the ability to provide content in a digital world with delivery platforms with an almost-unlimited content capacity, some of the interviewees talked about the changes that would need to be made to regulatory practice to reflect these changes. The need for the audience to rely increasingly on its own judgements, rather than those of an external statutory body, would become more and more important:

> I think in very broad terms it's true to say that...people seem to be seeing online as quite a different environment. They do understand that it is essentially unregulated and therefore there is a different set of expectations that occurs and I think that's fair to say in terms of new media platforms being perceived differently by the public.
>
> (Alison Preston, Senior Research Associate, Ofcom, UK)

Nonetheless, there was still a role for the law and for self-regulation:

> One of the things I find interesting, in the rather technophilic frame within which the discussion about regulating the media industries since the Internet has proceeded, is that the fact that all regulatory structures will inevitably have weaknesses and limitations is considered to be a sufficient basis to laugh out of court any potential future regulation of these industries and indeed of the Internet. One doesn't have to look further than the much vaunted competition regulation at the heart of Ofcom and EU media regulation to see how imperfect regulation can be. So that technophilic frame doesn't obviate the bigger issue: that one can still, in fact, attempt to implement reasonably effective controls and have sanctions for transgressions, and that these are likely to have significant effects.
>
> (Georgina Born, Cambridge University, UK)

Self-restraint too had a role:

> I think this is quite an interesting moment that it is probable that we are talking more about a world where rather than regulation acting in a censorship role, getting rid of stuff, you may want to continue to have interventions to create safe havens. You know, CBBC [BBC digital children's channel] on the Web should be a place where you

can let your children go and they won't come up with anything horrible. And, secondly, that you will want to, and it's quite a good world for public service broadcasters potentially, to focus quite hard on the 'demand' side and on media literacy (a slightly sinister phrase, but an important topic). In other words, both inside formal education, but more broadly, it is making tools available to the public and also in a sense just engaging the public in thinking hard about media. I think we are entering a world where censorship is going to be technically extremely hard to achieve and, secondly, may not feel desired, in societal terms. I mean we reached the point in the mid-nineties with feature films, properly labelled, shown at different times of the day, where the number of people who complained that content had been edited were greater than the people who didn't. And that indeed is the way the world is moving. And that suits us.

(Mark Thompson, BBC, UK)

Bill Bush cautioned against accepting the inevitability of change earlier than was necessary. He argued that the regulator had to be careful that it was not a catalyst for changes in the industry ahead of their time. When discussing the diminution of ITV's public service obligations, for example, he said that he thought Ofcom had been hasty in allowing changes that could have been made later when the direction of the market was clearer.

We were surprised at the speed at which Ofcom let ITV off the hook. I think at the time we thought that there was fairly obviously a five to seven years' trajectory, so, yes, in the run-up to switchover, ITV would have to be increasingly let off the hook. We thought that position (would be) reached over a five-year period, in fact it was reached right at the beginning of the five-year period. but Ofcom's analysis (was) a very pessimistic view . . . okay, it was going to take some years to develop and as it developed you could progressively release ITV from its obligations.

In general, he said, it was best to wait:

[Regarding the future of commercial public service broadcasting] it's a problem which will need to be solved when it's clearer what the available solutions might be. But (it is better to) try to future-fix at a point where a fix is not necessary than (when) the future is so cloudy that the likelihood of making a mistake is too big.

The United States

A brief history

To an extent which might surprise a modern-day observer of American broadcasting in its early years, a significant part of the stage was set not by commerce but by academic institutions and other noncommercial interests. They saw in the wireless the means of building a democratic culture and bringing the benefits of education to a much wider audience, triumphing over some of the problems created by America's great distances. Out of these perspectives grew a concept of public broadcasting, initially concerned with the transmission of educational programming, but moving on later to a wider range of output, always on a shoestring. When the first radio licensing law was enacted in 1912, among the applicants were the operators of nearly a thousand transmitters, many of them with educational concerns. Besides those who legitimated themselves, there were numerous others who failed to do so and continued to broadcast, for the moment unchecked.[31]

When the US entered the war in 1917, all these activities were either closed down or taken over by the US Navy. Following the Armistice in the following year, much of the credit for a wide range of technical developments during the war was given to the US Navy, leading the House of Representatives to give serious consideration to proposals that the Navy should be in charge of all broadcasting. It would enjoy a monopoly for which, proponents of the idea claimed, radio was naturally suited. The popularity of monopolies outside the US was demonstrated in Europe, where their role in building or rebuilding national unity was clear.

In the US, however, the notion of a monopoly, especially one with an implication of government involvement, attracted challenges from suspicions born of native instinct and from the more practical prospect of a possible conflict with anti-trust legislation. Nevertheless, the thought of a private monopoly provoked less controversy. An approach was made to the four major companies involved in the industry with the suggestion that they might jointly resolve the issue, so keeping monopoly power out of the hands of government.[32] The market would be divided between them. At the time, their primary concern was not with broadcasting in the sense we now know it. Their objective was the dominance of international communications by wireless telephony, reducing the power of the international cable companies. However, they were aware that their neat arrangements for parcelling the future out between them were being bypassed by the so-called 'amateurs' who were creating their own technical equipment and putting it to work. These activities, growing in scale and confidence, prompted the big companies to complain about the violation of their patents and the development of an industry unregulated by either commercial agreements or the law.

The responsibility for resolving the many problems which were accumulating lay with Herbert Hoover, the Secretary for Commerce, but the extent to which he had powers to impose solutions was uncertain. The first Washington Radio Conference in February, 1922, an assembly of representatives from industry, agencies and the amateurs, resolved that he should be given whatever was needed for effective regulation of the competing interests. However, the draft law which was prepared could make only limited headway in the face of the belief that Hoover, whose presidential aspirations were known, might abuse the fresh powers it would have given him.

Hoover called a second Conference in the capital a year later. It ended with another resolution, more robust than its predecessor and asserting its belief that the Secretary did, indeed, have the authority needed to clear the confusion which infested the industry. Many companies contended with their neighbours, threatening to drown out their signals by increasing the power of their transmissions. Hoover began to reallocate spectrum, splitting it into three bands: In the top band were higher-powered stations serving large areas without interference from neighbours, followed by those placed in the second band: middle-powered stations in smaller areas and again without interference, but not necessarily without some time sharing. Finally, in the third band were the low-powered stations all broadcasting on 360 metres in limited areas and mainly restricted to daytimes when interference was less. Educational stations, in the third band, suffered badly under the scheme.

Immediately before the second Radio Conference, the first steps had been taken to seek revenue from advertising in programmes. The hostility which had been expressed towards advertising at the first Conference was now less strident. AT & T's 'toll broadcasting' appeared first, encouraging anyone and everyone to buy the right to address the public. Advertising appeared more frequently with its financial significance growing. In 1926 the first of the major networks was launched when the Radio Corporation of America founded the National Broadcasting Corporation (NBC).

The continuing calls for a regulatory authority were eventually answered. Hoover's allocation of frequencies had been successfully challenged in the courts and he was forced to abandon it. That prompted the Radio Act of 1927, built on the bones of the failed 1922 draft. It established a five-strong Federal Radio Commission, given the right to grant licences on a standard of 'public interest, convenience, and necessity' which, lifted from utilities legislation, has proved itself a leitmotif throughout eight decades of American broadcasting. The Act banned monopolies and, reflecting the First Amendment to the Constitution, also banned censorship. In the same year, NBC, which ran two networks, a 'Blue' and a 'Red', was joined by the Columbia Broadcasting System, with a further network, the Mutual Broadcasting System, opening in 1934.[33] At no opportune time was there talk of a National Broadcaster.

The future President Roosevelt, on taking office as Secretary of Commerce in 1933, set up a Commission to examine the communications industry across the nation, with the object of assuming federal control through a new regulator. This resulted in the Communications Act of 1934, with the Federal Radio Commission reappearing as the Federal Communications Commission (FCC), consisting of seven members appointed by the President, with the ruling Party having a majority and taking the Chair. An amendment intended to protect the educational non-profit-making stations by, among other things, allowing them to sell airtime was defeated in the Senate.

The outcome was to leave commercial interests in the ascendant, as it turned out, until the present day. The educational channels struggled on, attracting small audiences to programmes which were regularly produced with very limited resources. Access granted by the FCC in 1945 to a number of FM channels and permission in 1946 to non-commercial educational stations to operate at 10 watts or less failed to provide much additional impetus because the take-up of FM itself was generally slow.

Television made its debut at the New York World Fair in 1939. Its fortunes during the war were chequered, with restrictions on sponsorship and advertising introduced long before the US entered the war, followed by reductions in daily transmission hours, both imposed by the FCC. Only weeks after the US had declared war on Japan in 1941 a voluntary system of censorship was set up. Erik Barnouw has provided a valuable analysis of the commercial fortunes of broadcasting during the war, when radio was the dominant medium.[34] Companies in 1939 were accustomed to selling only about a third of their available advertising time, giving over the unsold time to a variety of material sufficiently uncommercial to suggest a genuine dialogue with the audience. Manufacturers and other advertisers, deprived of consumer goods to sell, chose to place brief corporate messages instead and to seek out cultural and other material which would enhance their prestige. While the atmosphere of fervid commercialism was tempered, the networks built up their news services and drew in very large numbers of viewers.

When the war ended in 1945, a number of America's largest cities either lacked a television station or were less well provided than some of their contemporaries. The FCC, confronting a very large number of demands for frequencies, was obliged in 1948 to announce a freeze on allocations which was to last until 1950. Advertisers were not the only interested group campaigning for a thaw. Educational broadcasters formed another. Their progress was uncertain. In 1950 the Ford Foundation, out of two funds, for the Advancement of Education and for Adult Education, made a grant of $50,000 to the Joint Committee on Educational Television to finance the lobbying of the FCC for spectrum. The result was the Commission's decision to put aside 162 UHF channels and 80 VHF channels for the use of non-commercial educational television services. However, by 1960 only 60 stations were on the air against an allocation by then of 257 channels. There were reservations in the academic community about the pressures which might follow federal funding. However, Congress, under the 1962 Educational Television Facilities Bill, created a five-year plan to give $32 million to new facilities. A proposal for a Presidential Commission to study the subject of educational broadcasting was followed up and funded by the Carnegie Foundation. The report of its Commission spoke of public television, treating educational programming as a subset and describing it as including all that is of human interest and importance, but not at present available for support by advertising and not arranged for formal instruction. Its suggestion that a new corporation should be funded by a receiving licence was not pursued. The eventual result was the formation of the Corporation for Public Broadcasting (CPB) in 1967, under which the Public Broadcasting Service (PBS) and National Public Radio (NPR) were developed. With the acceptance by the President and Congress of that idea and federal funding pledged in support, a cornerstone had been laid for public broadcasting; not a very grand one in economic terms, but a clear assertion of values other than those of the market.

There were two particular characteristics of American broadcasting in the period which followed. The first was the huge rise in American television production which increasingly dominated overseas markets with both cultural and economic consequences in those markets. This process was to coincide, as time passed, with the development of a global market in a very wide range of products. The second was the domestic phenomenon of changes in ownership. Large companies took over smaller companies until they were themselves swallowed up by even larger companies. Finally, the broadcasting media ended up in the hands of a small group of vast corporations, their interests often far removed from the business of information, education and entertainment. The consequence has been a chilling effect, capable of discouraging the proper scrutiny in the public interest of controversial subjects. The result of that has been the muting of the democratic dialogue outside the public broadcasting channels and they too have not been immune from the pressures that arise from the shortage of funding.

It is into this considerable gap that the new media have moved, bypassing their older rivals and enabling voices and expressions of opinions which have been denied access to the mainstream media. The problems remain of devising suitable means by which the debates they stimulate can be channelled into the greater debate in the public sphere, the place where democracy can live or die. Encountered in each of the societies in this study, they are not made easier by the growing penetration of the new media by the same commercial interests which are active in the mainstream.

Cable television

Cable television made a modest start in the mid-twentieth century as the means of improving reception of television in poorly-served areas, often by placing an aerial on a high point and distributing the signal from there to the surrounding districts. The next step was the distribution of signals received over long distances, provoking opposition from established television stations and leading the FCC to ban the practice. The Commission also placed limits on the kinds of programmes the cable operators could relay, but in the early 1970s there were counter-moves to remove such restrictions, encouraging investment. The year 1972 saw the launch of Home Box Office (HBO), the first national cable network. The introduction of satellite transmissions stimulated further growth in the industry, producing nearly 80 networks at the start of the 1990s. The 1996 Federal Telecommunications Act followed deregulatory principles, promoting the use of broadband and, later, the development of digital cable to meet an increasing demand for high-definition television and television-on-demand.

Cable is now the principal means of reception in the US. Estimates vary and the true figure may be higher or lower than that of 58 percent of television households given by the National Cable Television Association on its website.[35] Costs to subscribers vary according to the contents of the package of programmes they choose. Some services carry advertising, but others, at the high-end of the market where the signals are encrypted, do not do so.

Legislation

Three Acts dominate American broadcasting:

The Radio Act, 1927

It established the Federal Radio Commission with five members with powers to grant, deny or remove radio licences and to assign frequency and power levels for every licence. It was forbidden to exercise any censorship.

The Communications Act, 1934

It replaced the Radio Commission with a Federal Communications Commission. It introduced a standard for the granting of licences, namely 'public interest, convenience, and necessity'.

The Telecommunications Act, 1996

The goal of the new Act, as described by the FCC, was to let anyone enter any communications business and it had 'the potential to change the way we work, live and learn'. It contained guidelines for obscenity and violence in respect of cable and satellite channels. It outlined the granting and licensing of broadcast spectrum by the government, the use of revenues generated by licensing, the terms of licences and their renewal processes.

Institutions

The Federal Communications Commission

1. *Constitution.* Created under the 1934 Communications Act to replace the Federal Radio Commission, the Commission currently has 5 members, appointed by the President. No party may have more than 3 members. It has a Managing Director. The staff is divided into 7 operating bureaux and 10 offices. The bureaux include a Consumer and Governmental bureau and bureaux for Enforcement, Wireless Telecommunications, and Public Safety and Homeland Security. Offices include those of the General Counsel, Media Relations, Communications Business Opportunities and Engineering and Technology.

2. *Interpretations of the public interest*

The new Commission inherited from its predecessor the criterion for the awarding of licences: to be given only if they could be perceived to serve the public interest, convenience and necessity. 'Convenience' and 'necessity' waned in significance as time passed and only 'the public interest', despite passing through many changing interpretations has remained a factor in the American broadcasting debate – 'the Blue Book', encouragement of diversity, relaxation of ownership rules, the lifting of format regulation.

The FCC declared, shortly after the passage of the Act, that it would apply the test to issues of content as well as to technical matters. In doing so, it would set the public's interest, convenience and necessity above that of the broadcaster or the advertiser. As it had explained in 1929, it was using a measure to evaluate licence applications and renewals in which music, classical and light, religion, education, important public events, discussions of public questions, news and matters of interest to all the family were included. The word 'entertainment' did not appear.

In 1946 the FCC released a report by its staff on the public service responsibilities of licensees, known as the Blue Book from the colour of its cover. For the previous few years, licence renewals had been dependent on reports from the Commission's engineers without any indication of content or performance. There was a growing sense that standards had been slipping over a lengthy period and, within the FCC itself, a feeling had developed that far too little attention was being paid to 'promise and performance'. The report, self-critical of the staff in some respects, detailed extensive shortcomings among the licensees; for instance, the imbalance in staffing and remuneration between a few programme-makers and many salespeople who on average were paid almost three times as much. There were large differences in the earnings of company salesmen and the creative talent they hired. Coverage of public affairs was said to have declined strikingly. The report set out four factors influencing the FCC's attitude to renewals: a not-excessive use of advertisements, discussions of local issues, live local programmes and the broadcasting of unsponsored programmes. The Commission had evidence of malpractice among the stations in recording their outputs, undercounting commercials or playing an excessive number of gramophone records. The appearance of the report, which was neither endorsed nor rejected by the FCC, aroused a major controversy, led by the National Association of Broadcasters (NAB). The charge against the Commission was one of censorship contrary to the Communications Act. Some years before the full fury of the McCarthy hearings broke, the Commissioners and a British contributor to the report were denounced as Communists. In the face of these attacks, despite some initially robustly defiant statements, the FCC's resolution quailed and the impact of the Blue Book was minimised and then forgotten. It was not until 1960 that another interpretation of the public interest was issued by the Commission. The catalogue of desirable output varied little from that issued in 1929, with two significant differences: the addition of entertainment programmes and editorialising by licensees. (The Commission's role in the evolution of the Fairness Doctrine between the early 1940s and its ending in the late 1980s is described on pp. 72–73 of Chapter 3.)

Under President Reagan (1981–1989) the FCC promoted a policy of deregulation, described by its Chairman as setting the broadcasters free. Ownership rules were a particular target for relaxation and the public interest played only a minor role in the work of the Commission at that time. The notable exception to that was an increasing concern over obscenity, a preoccupation which has continued to dominate the Commission's activities under subsequent administrations.

3. *Accountability of the FCC*

Asking questions about the different forms of accountability which might be expected of the Commission, the interviewer raised first the question of how its accountability to Congress worked in practice. Rick Chessen, an Adviser to Commissioner Copps of the FCC, said that

Formally, it means obviously that they control our budget and that can be a very powerful tool. They pass the laws that keep us accountable, if we don't do something that they like, they can always pass statutes, and they have certainly done that .... Then there are formal oversight hearings which happen periodically. So we have two committees that oversee us. Generally, the Commerce Committee in the Senate and the House Commerce Committee. Within those, there are Telecommunications sub-committees but, generally, the Commerce Committee in the House and the Senate, those are the committees that generally have oversight over the Commission and we go up to both in the process of re-authorising, getting our budget. The Commissioners can also go up to testify if the committees are interested in particular topics. Recently there's been notices of some hearings on media ownership that the Senate would like to have. There have also been hearings on digital television. Sometimes they call up the Chair, sometimes they call up all five [Commissioners] and they answer questions. Then there are ongoing dialogues, I would say more informally, with the Hill .... It (is) also a way that a lot of a groups and industry also can work Congress, to ask them to send letters to the FCC and often provide them with drafts. And so it's another lobbying tool in some ways but Congressional members themselves also have a real interest in these areas. And they have their own staffs and they are often in contact with us, not only on general topics but even as individual orders come up.

What obligations might it have to the public?

There are certain requirements we have under the Administrative Procedures Act to make sure the public has an opportunity to comment. Anytime we adopt a rule it has to be made public, the public has a chance to participate. They can do it electronically and some of our docket, say, about media ownership, there's tens of thousands of comments. Now, the GAO [the Government Accountability Office] recently took the FCC to task a little bit (because) there's an inside-Washington crowd that tends to have access to more information about the process than the public.

Were there areas which, if he were redrafting the legislation, he would want to include?

One of the things we've done recently is disclosure of stations' public files on the Internet. I think shining the light of day on what people are doing will have a beneficial impact. Right now it's very difficult for people to know what their station is doing. The stations keep that information at the station in a file, how they are serving the public, but nobody ever looks at it. The station would have a heart attack if anybody showed up to actually look at the file. Hopefully, having a form that is standardised and is on the Internet that would disclose what people are doing will be very helpful. There are many broadcasters that are doing a good job but then there's some that aren't, but finding out who those stations are is difficult. There are watchdog groups that could probably do a good job but they can't get the data unless they go to every station in the country and they just don't have the resources. Disclosure could have a terrific effect because then, even if you didn't have formal requirements, you could show the world here are the broadcasters that are doing news, here are the ones that are covering their local communities, and here are the ones who are just running infomercials all day.

The next question concerned the accountability of the Commission's licensees beyond that which they had to the Commission itself.

Well, there's a formal requirement that they serve the needs and interests of the local community. Now, during the 1980s, the Commission basically took the position that the market place is the best way to achieve that goal. So now, other than children's programming, there's very little at this point that the local community knows they can expect from licensees.

In Philadelphia, Monroe Price, at the University of Pennsylvania, spoke of the FCC's accountability to the courts:

It would be accountability, in addition to Congress, to the federal courts, ultimately to the Supreme Court. There's a definite dialogue between the FCC and the courts and in a way the Supreme Court is behind it because if the dialogue goes off kilter then the Supreme Court will take the case and say to the intermediate court, 'you've gone too far, you've misunderstood any kind of cues about what your relationship to the FCC should be'. So a lot of the debate has been about evidence. I think about whether the FCC has had sufficient grounding for its decisions... it's about process often, maybe there are other things at stake but often about process and about evidence for conclusions. So if the FCC says cable operators can only have 27 percent of the national market, a court might say how did you get at that figure as opposed to 35 percent. And so while there may be a mass of other kinds of intervention, one function of the court has been, in theory, to make the FCC more like Ofcom purports to be, an evidence-based policy decision-making authority. And you could argue that it's designed to make it less political but it may also be because the court, to the extent that it's conservative, thinks that there's no evidence for very much regulation so that the more you require to justify a regulation, the less regulation there'll be.

He was asked how transparent he believed the FCC to be:

I think that there's definitely a feeling that there are decisions that are made that are political not in a horrible sense, but in an American sense of the term. They're political in the sense that guys sit together and they make a deal or the Commissioners among themselves make a deal and in that sense the evidence is helpful. This is one of the problems of the FCC. It's a kind of, it plays both these roles. It looks like an administrative agency, but it acts in a very political way. Here, it's sort of weird what the word 'political' means. Can you be independent and political? And I think they think they can be. The whole structure or the appointments is based on a particularly US administrative meaning of 'independence' in which Commissioners have a structure of independence but they seem to be intensely ideology-based or party-related.

The FCC, broadcast news and the workings of the market

As what can strike non-Americans as a paradox, the FCC has found it impossible on First Amendment grounds to require its licensees to provide news broadcasts, although many stations transmit news summaries and longer bulletins as attractive to their publics and commercially sustainable. The treatment of news was put to Reed Hundt, a former Chair of the FCC, in a conversation which began with his agreement that the FCC had a poor record in looking forward:

> The FCC is famously bad at looking forward with accuracy. It's famous for looking forward with a bad pair of glasses.
> Interviewer: And the other suggestion is the glasses it looks forward with are very industry tinted.
> Hundt: So you take the two things, you add them together and you've got the whole answer. The right answer is usually the opposite of whatever it does and the looking forward is usually wrong. But it is certainly true the FCC has a way to ignore the present.

When he had been Chair, what had he done about changing the FCC?

> Everything. We tried to change everything. Once we figured out the two rules I just told you, we tried to change everything. We espoused the following. A monumental indifference to all predictions about technology and a general view that if we were extremely clear about our goals, we would be rather likely, but never certain, to accomplish those goals. And both things in my judgment served us well ... You know, why is it the case that if you're pretty clear about the goals, you'll probably more or less succeed. Because the clearer you are in regulation about the goals, the more likely it is in a democracy that the public opinion will support you.

Bill Buzenberg, of the Center for Public Integrity, catalogued some of the losses which he believed reliance on the market had produced:

The truth is public service broadcasting has largely been given over to the free market. What's the free market going to do? They're going to go for biggest audience they can create which means entertainment and sports. These are simply worth more money. Look at all of the news organisations who are now controlled by big entertainment and sports companies in effect. Their interest is not public service journalism, educating citizens in a democracy. It used to be that public service role was central to these companies. The old CBS believed in public service journalism. That was what CBS did in exchange for getting free use of the public's airwaves. There is not quite the same ethos today. Yes, journalism makes money, too, because it creates an audience, but the more entertaining the news is, the bigger audience it creates and the more money it makes. Public service journalism is important in society to educate citizens about the things they need to know. You won't get publicly traded conglomerates that own media companies like General Electric or Disney to speak out about their role in educating citizens in a democracy.

The Corporation for Public Broadcasting

The circumstances surrounding the formation of the Corporation (CPB) have already been described. Congress declared that it was in the public interest for the federal government to encourage the growth and development of public radio and public television, including the use of such media for instructional, educational and cultural purposes. The new body was also declared not to be an agency or an establishment of the US government.

The CPB is headed by a Board of 9 directors appointed by the President on the advice and with the consent of the Senate. No more than 5 of the members may come from a single party. They should be eminent in such fields as education, cultural and civic affairs or in the Arts, including radio and television. They should be representative, as nearly as practicable, of various regions of the country, professions and occupations. One member is to represent the licensees and permittees of the public television stations and one to represent the licensees and permittees of the public radio stations.

The Corporation's mission statement

Adopted on 13 July 1999 by the CPB Board of Directors, the statement runs as follows:

The Corporation for Public Broadcasting is a private, nonprofit corporation created by Congress in 1967. The mission of CPB is to facilitate the development of, and ensure universal access to, non-commercial high-quality programming and telecommunications services. It does this in conjunction with non-commercial educational telecommunications licensees across America. The fundamental purpose of public telecommunications is to provide programs and services which inform, enlighten and enrich the public. While these programs and services are provided to enhance the knowledge, and citizenship, and inspire the imagination of all Americans, the Corporation has particular responsibility to encourage the development of programming that involves creative risks and that addresses the needs of unserved and underserved audiences, particularly children and minorities. The Corporation is accountable to the public for investing its funds in programs and services which are educational, innovative, locally relevant, and reflective of America's common values and cultural diversity. The Corporation serves as a catalyst for innovation in the public broadcasting industry, and acts as a guardian of the mission and purposes for which public broadcasting was established.

Ben Scott, Policy Director of Free Press, a Washington-based advocacy group, spoke as a supporter of the public broadcasters. He thought of them

...as partners as opposed to competitors. There are people particularly in our community who think that public broadcasting has basically just foundered under the political pressure of don't do anything controversial, don't take on the Congress, don't speak truth to power because if you do it will turn around and take your money and make you disappear. Our view is we have to build a political will to insulate public broadcasting from political pressure as it was intended when it was created in the 1960s. Public broadcasting should aspire to realise the vision that lawmakers had, put it in place and then expand its service offerings so that it appeals to a wider cross section of the American public. Right now public broadcasting, because it's backed into a financial corner, is forced to target its programming on those viewers who can write cheques. Pledge drives. Much of their money comes from that. They have no choice but to do that. So they're stuck. They make programming decisions that are cautious. They don't do all the kinds of programmes that we think they should but our view is that largely the situation is not of their own making.

The Public Broadcasting Service

The Public Broadcasting Service (PBS) was set up in 1969 as a non-profit-making corporation. Its members are the public television stations in the US, numbering 355 at the time of writing. They are held by a total of 168 non-commercial, educational licensees, 86 of which are community associations, 56 are academic institutions, 20 are state authorities and the remaining 6 are local educational or municipal authorities.

It does not itself transmit nor produce programmes, but acquires programmes from a variety of sources. These are in turn distributed to individual stations in return for payments. Heavily dependent on funding from the public, a proportion of the Service's income comes in the form of grants from the CPB. The Corporation's own government funding has been under threat in recent years as the Administration sought additional support for the wars in Iraq and Afghanistan.

PBS is watched each week by about 73 million people in some 46 million households while, over a month, approximately 125 million people view the service. The PBS website (www.pbs.org) is one of the most-visited in the US.

The PBS's Ombudsman

Michael Getler (PBS's Ombudsman) explained how his post had been created following the report of an independent review of editorial practices in the service:

> ...one of the chief recommendations was that PBS have an Ombudsman to enhance the, you know, the cliché words, which are 'transparency' and 'accountability'. I was, at the time, the Ombudsman for the Washington Post and I'd been there for 5 years as Ombudsman, which was much longer than I had signed on for. And that was coming to an end, my contract was, so Pat Mitchell, who was then the President of PBS, approached me and said, would I come and do the same thing at PBS. It sounded like a good way to stay engaged, so I did that.

> Interviewer: What I'd be interested in knowing is how are the complaints different for the Washington Post or for a press publication compared with PBS?
>
> Getler: They're similar in some ways. One of the reasons I took (the PBS job) is that PBS and the Washington Post are both in their own way very important organisations, very important to informing the

public, very important in a democracy to have an informed citizenry. That sounds corny but it's true...The Post has good readers and PBS has good viewers and they're smart. There are a lot of people out there who make very interesting, unique observations about what they see and hear on TV and read in print or on the web. So they both are important. They both have very high standards and they both need to live up to them. Ombudsmen can help in that role....

He makes no formal reports to anyone at PBS, but gives his assessment of the current state of mind among the public through a weekly column published online. The column is also widely read within PBS by staff and management. Although the Ombudsman's column is meant primarily for viewers, Getler said it also amounts to an internal handbook for PBS management about things that can and do go wrong. There is no other mechanism, he says, within PBS where these missteps are shared and can serve as warning signals for others. Emphasising that there was no collusion between PBS and the FCC in the handling of complaints, Michael Getler said that he had, early in his tenure, written a column criticising the Commission for its action in penalising a small college station. Just one viewer had written to complain about foul language and the FCC had imposed a fine. He thought it was a disproportionate reaction to a single complaint, even though he considered the bad language artistically indefensible in the context.

National Public Radio

The launch of PBS in 1969 was followed, a year later, by the appearance of National Public Radio (NPR). In contrast to PBS, NPR was to be a broadcaster. Now, in the first decade of the twenty-first century, it offers a service to more than 25 million people from more than 800 stations across the country. To a radio community where a senior executive of one of the largest chains of stations could say 'We're not in the business of informing our listeners, we're in the business of making money', PBS's hour-long news has appeared as a kind of nightly rebuke to those values. Ben Scott, of Free Press, an advocacy group based in Washington but with countrywide support, described the difficulties of funding NPR and PBS.

We've looked at a variety of proposals for how to increase the funding in US public broadcasting. I think we spend about a dollar per capita on public broadcasting versus the UK fee per year. An incredible disparity and if you ask people whether they think the tax dollar in public broadcasting is a good investment, it's an 80 percent favourable rating. It's unheard of. You can't get 80 percent of Americans to agree about anything. They all support public broadcasting, even if they don't watch it. And I think the great irony about public media right now is that everybody thinks it's a good idea but nobody watches it. What I mean is that it's not clear that nobody would pay for it. It is a sense in the Congress that big dollars for public media is a third rail. Partly that is pressure from commercial media saying, 'don't give money to public broadcasting because then you're subsidising our competitor'. And so there's pressure not to give money but when they do give money and public broadcasting is successful, then they say, 'okay cut the funding from those guys because they're competing with us'. Well there's sort of a catch-22 there. Either you get money and you do well and you're competing or you don't get money and you don't do well and you can't compete. How do you create a non-commercial sector that's valuable in the media system for citizens? That requires a political will to recognise that the marketplace is not the only mechanism for delivering content.

WETA: A public broadcasting station

One of the main pillars of public broadcasting is WETA, a radio and television station in Washington since 1952. Its operations are now addressed to a steadily increasing audience which, through streaming on the web, extends far beyond the station's birthplace. Mary Stewart, Vice-President of Communications at WETA, described the business of the station:

In the United States among the public broadcasting stations, WNET in New York and WGBH in Boston are the two stations that produce the most for the system. We are the third-largest producing station for the PBS system. And people tend to wind up with specialties: We do productions with Ken Burns, a film-maker we've worked with for over 20 years including the most recent large production he did with Lynn Novick on World War II, titled *The War*. We produce *The NewsHour with Jim Lehrer* every weeknight and *Washington Week* with Gwen Ifill weekly. Based in the nation's capital, WETA has a particular opportunity to produce public affairs specials and series. We also create performance specials from our major national venues. Those three areas [history, public affairs, performance] tend to be the main things that we do – we don't currently produce any drama – but we produce about two-dozen specials each year in addition to our continuing series and cover a wide range of genres.

Interviewer: So you'd buy that in?

Stewart: We don't have to buy it individually. We pay dues to PBS based on our station size and market size and station strength. That's how the dues are assessed in a complicated pattern, and we get access to the prime time schedule and to many other scheduling services. We can then adapt that or augment it, so we and every other PBS station are going to have *Antiques Roadshow* at 8 o'clock on Mondays. Our local programmer might decide that just really is not the time he wants to run it, he runs it at 9. He can do that within a complicated rule system of how much we have to comply with common carriage. There are certain hours that he wants to fill other ways, for instance late Friday evenings and most weekend hours. Now as we all transition more into the digital multi-cast era, there are shared streams of programming that many of the stations might be using, PBS Kids, how-to channels, documentary channels, etc. that aren't all individually programmed. At WETA, we may programme these ourselves for our local audience, but we are a larger station than most.

She was asked how she defined the public interest.

Generally our mission, we believe, is to try to take the high road with programming and do those things which are not lowest common denominator but highest common denominator.

Interviewer: You mean quality?

Stewart: Quality is such a subjective assessment. There are certainly people who think we should be serving whatever niche is not being served; and that goal was most clear in the early days of public broadcasting. Nobody else was doing kids and the eclectic kind of programming that early public television – and especially early public radio – were doing. Early public television was doing cooking shows and exercise shows and science for children and teacher and how-to painting shows... unheard of. Now there are whole cable channels devoted to specific genres, with more to come with multicast digital services. What we have kept as our guide post is trying to find and create programming that serves the audience in an educational and/or enlightening way, to inspire lifelong learning by curious people of all walks of life. They – the individuals throughout our society who want to watch and listen to programming that is created to satisfy that curiosity and aspiration for something meaningful in their media – are the people to whom we are beholden.

Had the latest switch proved to be a good decision?

> Our ratings have gone up from being a 1.8 when we were news or a hybrid station to being 4.8, which is high for us or for anyone in this market. It took a time, however, for the membership contributions to catch up proportionally, but they have. That lag is typical, and in fact we had less of a lag with this change to classical than the industry expectation of three years. As a listener or viewer, you probably are with us for a while before you decide to give to us; and even the most successful stations, television or radio, tend to have contributions from only about a tenth to a fifteenth of the actual users.

A little further into the conversation, she spoke about the values of public broadcasting, referring particularly to radio:

> On radio, we are serving a niche that would otherwise be a void in our market in terms of commercial or public broadcasting; we are now the only classical music station. It was an easy decision, because we were in our hearts classical broadcasters for so long, and we can't help but believe it is a true broadcasting good that you are sharing a free art form with people and introducing them to it or acquainting them with it or letting them enjoy it through a service they would not otherwise get. Radio's maturation to me is clearer than television's. Television has had its own comeuppance – radio had television come in but television had cable come in. And all of a sudden, public television, which used to be the fairly exclusive purveyor of kids, history, how-to and science and most drama, had competition. But with all of the cable and now multicast services coming in, there is presumably a lot more competition for our viewership. Our donors still tell us there's something distinctly different about public broadcasting's quality, that they are essentially now asking us to be a trusted editor in the media world of overwhelming choice. Sure I could go watch a channel devoted to one topic but I don't want to do that. I want you to choose the best history programme, or the best biography, or the best science programme; and I like the mixed schedule. How the multicast environment changes that, is yet to be seen.

The National Association of Broadcasters

The National Association of Broadcasters (NAB) was formed in 1923 as a defensive move by the industry against the claims of ASCAP (American Society for Composers, Authors and Publishers) for copyright fees for the use of their members' music in programmes. The industry claimed that the composers benefited from the exposure, but the Supreme Court ruled against them. NAB was to champion the broadcasters in a number of brushes with the FCC in the succeeding years and it has traditionally been aggressive in defence of its members' interests. Perhaps the most notorious of the run-ins between the FCC and NAB occurred over the publication of the 'Blue Book' in 1945, following a period when mass renewals of licences was commonplace and accusations of falling standards were being levelled at the broadcasters. The incident is referred to on pp. 168–169.

A Washington DC broadcast attorney with experience of the NAB, an organisation with members located throughout the country, stressed the part that geography had played in the founding years of the American system:

> Some of the conception of what the public interest, convenience, necessity meant back in the 20s and 30s was also obviously a great concern with geographic distribution. (There was) the idea that this is a very big country. The US committed very early on not only to national services, obviously we have national networks that provide programming, but that the system would be a locally licensed system. There was great concern that when you were allocating licenses for radio stations there should be a fair geographic distribution so that all the radio stations would not end up just in the urban areas with the rest of the country left out.... there was geographic distribution at the beginning of the first service and all that was extremely important in the first several decades of the system because of the geographic distribution. Of course the Communications Act was written by Congressmen and Senators from all 50 states, that was obviously one of their overriding concerns. Like there was a specific section about geographic distribution of radio licenses that used to be huge, now that's a given.

She said that since 1996 the licence period for both radio and television has been 8 years. Although a few licences could be lost, in practice they were rare occasions. There were some petitions against renewal, but the FCC, with the First Amendment in mind, discounted those which were based on criticisms of content. There was now no competition for licences as there had once been, the courts being persuaded that the outcome was no better than if spectrum were auctioned. And auctions had now become the standard practice. The Commission's approval was needed before licences could change hands, but the process was very formal. There were some limited conditions to holding a licence:

Television broadcasters have to carry at least 3 hours a week of children's educational information programming... Broadcast does not receive as much First Amendment protection as other media. That may change given some recent court decisions, but that change will be by court decision. (There is) traditionally a stricture on indecency regulation. Just by market practice, broadcasters have also been, the programming on a broadcast station will not be as violent as programming on *Sopranos* [on HBO]. Or critically the premium pay per view type programming.... But that substantively is about it.

Interviewer: Because in the UK the regulator has restrictions on news and it has to be impartial and accurate and it has to be carried on public service broadcasting.

Interviewee: No, and the only thing that we used to have (in the US) but not any more, there used be something called the Fairness Doctrine. That broadcasters had to cover controversial issues of public importance and to cover such issues from various sides. That was such a morass, the FCC decided in 1987 no longer to enforce it and the FCC found it contrary to the First Amendment and actually contrary to the public interest because they found that it deterred broadcasters from covering controversial issues of public importance. It was going to lead to people clamouring to say, you didn't cover this side of this issue so therefore you need to have so and so to present this side of the issue and the FCC found that it actually inhibited public debate and the Doctrine was eliminated.

Advocacy groups

The role of advocacy groups in American life is much greater than in any of the other three countries in the study. In the US, the actions of the Executive Branch of government, which includes agencies like the FCC, are open to judicial review, creating opportunities for interventions by groups of which the Washington-based Media Access Project is one. Andy Schwartzman, its President, explained its origins:

A mentor of mine named Everett Parker pursued a case involving a racist television station in Jackson, Mississippi. And out of that came a decision that gave citizens the right to participate in FCC proceedings better as citizens. Prior to that time there was not such a right for legal standing. So in the wake of that, the creation of this right to participate, several organisations were formed to take advantage of that opportunity. Media Access Project was one of them. And its original focus at the time of its origin which was in 1971 was on seeking to assure adequate coverage of perspectives on the Vietnam War which was then underway. Out of a feeling that, today, what we would call the mainstream media, was not adequately portraying the full range of points and perspectives on the war.

Schwartzman was asked to describe how the Project worked:

We are an NGO which has some resemblance to advocacy groups that lobby and represent their membership before the Legislative Branch and the Executive Branch. We are not a membership group; we are a group of lawyers. We do not have any literal standing in the judicial sense, a right to participate or legitimate interest which would be cognisable by US courts as ourselves. We have clients. The clients are other organisations which have real live breathing members. Our clients are civil rights, civil liberties, consumer, environmental, labour, religious organisations, and they lack the resources of financial and technical, the expertise to participate in sophisticated public policy debate. Again in American terms, a company like Cisco has a Washington office which pursues the interests of Cisco with the government, legislative and executive branches. They also have law firms which are themselves lobbyists and advocates for their interests and who go to court for them. We view ourselves as the Washington law firm for these public interest organisations...They may be large and have substantial budgets, but they do not have the budget for telecommunications policy. We are foundation-funded: the Ford Foundation, the Macarthur Foundation, some individual family foundations.... these are non-profitable, charitable organisations which finance the bulk of our activities.

Ben Scott of Free Press outlined the role of his organisation:

Free Press reaches its membership through a website, a newsletter for subscribers, special messages for activists, the staging of public events, the writing of blogs, and town meetings at 6-8 week intervals throughout the country. For people wanting to approach the FCC or a Congressman, Free Press will supply text which is open to change even if the change represents something contrary to the organisation's agenda.

As for the membership, Ben Scott described it as a broad mix in age and colour. Every 18 months, Free Press holds a large-scale conference, which in January 2007 drew 3,500 people, about half its members, to Memphis.

Marcellus Alexander, Executive Vice-president of Television, NAB, looked at questions of funding from his perspective in a different part of the market from that which concerned most advocacy groups. Was the NAB serving viewers or, as advocacy groups claimed, only the shareholders?

> It is about both actually. Again, special interest groups and advocates miss a fundamental, economic fact. That is broadcasters compete with each other every minute of every day for viewers. So stations first serve their viewers, and by doing so, put themselves in position to fulfil their responsibilities to shareholders. Generating revenue for commercial broadcasters is made possible only after stations establish an audience and ratings of a size and demographic that is of interest to marketers. If programming content is not relevant to viewers in their local communities, they simply switch the channel and go to where they can find it. If the operator is not programming the station in a way that viewers want, that station is going to be out of business. It's as simple as that.

Complaints

Among the many possible forms of accountability, correspondence, emails and telephone calls from individual members of the public or from large groups play a significant role in the relationships of broadcasters and the management of new media with their publics. One of the major responsibilities of the PBS's Ombudsman Michael Getler is to deal with complaints. He said that they were all content-orientated.

> There's a fair amount of it which can be dealt with by just forwarding it directly to the station or to the producers or to viewer services here... I always ask the people that I forward this material to, I ask them 'could you please respond to this viewer and copy me?'. Let me know so that I get a sense of whether they've responded in a

substantive way or they're just trying to kiss them off. I think PBS does a fairly good job of responding at the level of stations, and the response as a whole, not always, is pretty good. There are a lot of those comments that you don't really want to write a column about, you just want somebody to take care of it and explain it and be aware that this aspect of their programme is raising questions. But what I try to do in my column is focus on the main journalistic issues raised by viewers in any week, or the most interesting observation that goes to the editorial standards of PBS, and write about that, and I deliver an independent assessment of those observations, independent of PBS and the viewers.

Interviewer: No sanctions (following complaints)?

Getler: Well, there have clearly been corrections on PBS. There have been new programmes commissioned to take a second look at a controversial subject. There have been websites revised that had misleading material.

A Washington DC Broadcast Attorney was asked whether the NAB handled complaints or simply forwarded them to the individual stations involved. Did any go on to the FCC?

No, I would say the vast majority of complaints go to the individual stations. Certainly if they are a very well run station, they will have a formal process for addressing and dealing with complaints and then obviously other types of complaints will go, and people will complain about various things, to the FCC.

Interviewer: Would the NAB provide information to its members on, say, the complaints procedure? Would you actually say this is best practice to best serve the viewer? Or is it not a relevant question because it's such a mature market?

Interviewee: (The NAB) provides lots of information on a lot of topics to its members . . . they've got handbooks for radio stations that cover everything from the basics on FCC regulation to all that kind of thing.

Mary Stewart described what happened to complaints directed to WETA, the radio and television PSB station in Washington:

If you didn't like the show you saw last night, you could certainly call us up. We have an audience service department in-house. At WETA, the audience service department types up daily reports and sends them around to all of us via email. We all study it nervously and joyously. And across the system, we share information about trends and highlights of our various reports. There are other mechanisms. For instance, people could register complaints with the FCC if they saw such content that they felt was indecent or offended them in other way. We might not hear about that for months if somebody sent in that. Such instances are extremely rare; perhaps most people call us directly.

Interviewer: So how long do you keep programmes for?

Stewart: Nowadays they're all digitally stored so it's different. Part of our clean-up day-to-day is tapes. But then the other piece of it is, and I'm glad you're talking with Michael [Getler], people complain to an Ombudsman to NPR or to PBS or to your own station. I would say in general I think that we do take complaints much more personally than some broadcasters...

Interviewer: When you say some broadcasters, you mean national broadcasters?

Stewart: Yes, they are national commercial networks; we are locally owned and operated stations sharing some programming nationally. Partly because of our own sensitivities to our local communities, the people calling you or writing you are the same ones who were or weren't going to pay $35 voluntarily to be our members. They're not filtered through the intermediary of an advertiser base. Our standards, however, can be difficult to achieve perfectly. I think both our audiences and we ourselves hold up this standard that sometimes it's just not realistic. Not every programme is going to be fabulous and a lot of debate is around the phrase 'fair, accurate and objective'. What do those mean to you? Are we talking about the individual programmes that have to be fair, accurate and objective or the collective scheduling? Is it tit for tat on a contentious issue? To some viewers, 'objective' is putting on your show that is kind of a strong point of view matched by putting a half-hour panel afterwards. The perception might be shaped by how we present the information. Do we say this one is 'point of view' programming or do we present a piece as from a journalist?... These nuances present very difficult questions especially in a more fractured media environment; and we discuss them and work with our producers and system to dissect them. I think it would be a shame if we felt like every programme had to be representing all sides of an issue – an impossibility. But we do believe that our programmes should bring up multiple viewpoints, make sure all statements and implications are fair and faithfully researched, and that the intent of the programme should be to amplify understanding of complex issues rather than narrow that perspective.

Future

In the other three countries under study, the outstanding future problems are the natures of regulation and funding for the public service institutions, all of which occupy dominant positions in the landscape of the countries' broadcasting. Regulation in the US insofar as, outside of indecency and obscenity, it exists in more than a formal sense, seems unlikely to be intensified to ensure the richer diversity of content which it is in the public interest to cultivate. Financial support for the relatively small proportion of public broadcasting in television and radio depends on three main sources: federal or state funding, grants from foundations of one kind of another and donations from corporations or concerned individuals. In the light of the financial crises besetting the US economy in 2008, all of these sources may be straitened for some time yet, whatever the outcome may turn out to be. The commercial sector too will be affected by the prevailing economic situation, threatening those niche channels which claim to be regarded as public broadcasting channels. The results of the approaching general election will almost certainly be influential, as will the continuing decline in newspaper circulations. At the moment of writing, the latter was affecting pressures within the FCC for a relaxation in media-ownership rules to allow an owner more than one licence in the same market as compensation for declining revenues. The consequences for freedom of expression of such a change could be considerable.

As the role of the Internet grows, blogs are likely to become even more numerous, threatening the tradition of impartiality which has been developed by some news broadcasters. Using what has become known as 'crowd sourcing', an apparently random gathering of the previously committed, to assert a truth about public opinion is a dangerous practice for the truth in news. And it is truthfulness there on which democracy in the US, as elsewhere, depends.

Notes

1. Inglis, K.S. *This is the ABC*, Black Inc., Sydney, 2006.
2. Turkey-slapping incident: a practice in which a boy rubs his genitals against a girl's face. It was not shown on mainstream television, but was streamed

on the Internet. It provoked a major outcry resulting in Parliament agreeing to extend some content restrictions to the Internet.

3. BBC Written Archive Centre, Caversham, UK.
4. *Connections Q1 2008*, CASBAA, 2008.
5. Broadcasting Bill, 1997
6. http://www.ddindia.gov.in/Information/Acts+And+Guidelines
7. The draft consultation bill can be seen at – http://mib.nic.in/informationb/POLICY/BROADCASTSERVICESREGULATIONBILL.htm
8. http://mib.nic.in/informationb/CODES/frames.htm
9. http://www.mib.nic.in/informationb/citizens.htm. The Charter also appears in Appendix iii.
10. http://www.ddindia.gov.in/Information/Citizen+Charter
11. http://www.allindiaradio.org/index.html
12. http://www.opsi.gov.uk/acts/acts2003/20030021.htm
13. http://www.ofcom.org.uk tv/ifi/codes/bcode/ofcom-broadcasting-code.pdf
14. http://www.ofcom.org.uk/tv/ifi/tvlicensing/guidance_notes_and_apps/tlcs/
15. http://www.ofcom.org.uk/tv/ifi/tvlicensing/guidance_notes_and_apps/notes/
16. www.atvod.co.uk
17. http://www.bbc.co.uk/bbctrust/assets/files/pdf/regulatory_framework/charter_agreement/bbcagreement_july06.pdf
18. http://www.bbc.co.uk/bbctrust/framework/charter.html
19. Ibid.
20. http://www.publications.parliament.uk/pa/ld200607/ldselect/ldcomuni/171/171.pdf
21. http://www.bbc.co.uk/bbctrust/assets/files/pdf/regulatory_framework/charter_agreement/royalchartersealed_sept06.pdf
22. http://www.bbc.co.uk/bbctrust/framework/purpose_remits.html
23. http://www.bbc.co.uk/bbctrust/framework/public_value_test/index.html
24. Barnett with Millwood Hargrave, 26 March 08.
25. Barnett, S. *Can the Public Service Broadcaster Survive? Renewal and Compromise in the New BBC Charter*, in Lowe, G.F. and Bardoel, J. *Public Service Broadcasting to Public Service Media*. RIPE@2007 Nordicom, 2008.
26. http://www.ofcom.org.uk/about/sdrp/
27. http://www.ofcom.org.uk/tv/psb_review/
28. http://www.ofcom.org.uk/consult/condocs/psb/psb/psb.pdf
29. Born, G. *Uncertain Vision: Birt, Dyke and the Reinvention of the BBC*. Secker and Warburg, London, 2004.
30. http://www.culture.gov.uk/NR/rdonlyres/096CB847-5E32-4435-9C52-C4D293CDECFD/0/CEPFeb2008.pdf
31. Barnouw, E. *History of broadcasting in the United States*, Vol. 1. p. 32, Oxford University Press, New York, 1966.
32. The Radio Corporation of America (RCA), General Electric, A.T. & T., and Westinghouse.
33. In 1943, NBC sold off the 'Blue' network which was relaunched as the American Broadcasting System (later known as ABC). MBS never followed the others into television and finally closed, after a sequence of different owners, in 1999.
34. Ibid, Vol. II. p. 337, Oxford University Press, New York, 1970.
35. http://www.ncta.com/Statistic/Statistic/Statistics.aspx

5
Conclusion

The countries reviewed

Australia, India, the UK and the US are all democracies, India the largest in the world. Three of them cover large stretches of territory, only the UK is small. India and the US have large populations, India the second largest in the world. The UK, a crowded group of islands, has, in comparison, a relatively small number of inhabitants, while Australia has, considering its land mass, a very small number. They share mixtures of indigenous and immigrant peoples, producing a variety of languages and differences in cultures of which broadcasters must take account. Solving the problems these raise is an important part of preserving and strengthening the national identity.

These countries all launched their broadcasting services with radio in the 1920s and radio remains important, especially so in India where television is not yet universally available. All four have an extensive range of commercial broadcasters, sustained by advertising or subscription. Three of the four have established traditions of public service broadcasting and created National Broadcasters to play a part in developing national cohesion. In the fourth, the US, there is a modest-sized public service operation in radio and television to which the government gives some support.

The UK is alone in funding one of its national public service broadcasters largely through a licence-fee levied on households equipped for television reception. A second publicly owned and non-profit-making television channel is funded by advertising revenue. In Wales, a third such organisation provides a digital service in Welsh and an analogue service in Welsh and English, drawing its revenue from a government grant and advertising. In Australia and India, the two national broadcasters are supported with public money, one of them also carrying advertising. Apart from federal support, American public broadcasters depend on grants from local states, donations from private corporations and foundations, and gifts from individuals for which the stations regularly campaign among their audiences.

India, where there is a long-running controversy over a programme standards code for broadcasters, remains the only country not yet to have converged its regulatory regimes. The US is unique in the tensions created by the First Amendment to the Constitution, which guarantees freedom of expression and has been subject to many differences of interpretation in the 80 years it has been applied to broadcasting.

New media have made considerable headway in three of the countries, with India's development slower for a number of reasons – economic, geographic and cultural – although the number of channels and services available to those that can receive (and afford) them is as great as in any other country considered here.

Accountability

As the previous chapter looking at each of the four countries under study showed, there is no clear definition of what accountability might be in terms of broadcasting nor, indeed, in terms of the digitalised post-broadcasting world, but there is a definite understanding that it is about processes and structures, both within and external to, organisations that can and should withstand scrutiny. The requirement for these processes start with the fact that a publicly owned medium – spectrum – is being used to transmit content, even post-digitalisation.

The scrutiny that is demanded comes from a variety of sources:

- government that frees up the spectrum for the delivery of audiovisual content
- regulatory structures that ensure the fair distribution of this commodity
- shareholders
- advertisers and other commercial interests
- audiences and users.

There are clearly different philosophies of accountability demanded from the commercial sector in comparison with the publicly funded institutions. The latter may receive direct public funding or it may receive indirect subsidies (such as reduced costs for access to spectrum). In the UK and in Australia public service broadcasters include commercial television companies, who have traditionally had access to subsidised spectrum for their free-to-air services in return for meeting certain programming obligations or requirements regarding access to content. The accountability of these organisations is thought by the interviewees as being to the audiences or users of the services, but their role is very specific and serves – and had to answer to – certain social needs. In India, in particular, the public service broadcaster sees its role as being a 'catalyst for social change' and a key variable to maintain the stability and cohesion of the nation. Many of the systems put in place to service this accountability are focused towards government and parliamentary processes; an argument being that the holders of these positions are elected representatives of the audience.

On the other hand, the commercial or private sector sees its accountability as being primarily to its shareholders. The way to meet this demand is to serve (and attract) those audiences and users that are appealing to advertisers, for example, thus bringing in revenue. Similarly, subscription services create a revenue line for shareholders and are a direct way of measuring how well a service is performing. In the US this more direct interaction is also to be found in the way public service broadcasters receive funding. The interviewee from WETA in the US likened the financial pledges made by viewers to WETA's services to the immediacy of a theatre audience clapping because they like a performance – or not.

Importantly, accountability is financial, whether it involves public monies or private monies. All the interviewees within organisations, and many who are observers of the industry, discussed accountability as a measure of how well resources are used. Economic theories and structures have been applied to many of the concepts formerly considered difficult to measure or quantify as a way of ensuring accountability. In the UK the BBC observes a series of criteria set out in its Charter that it must meet to fulfil its remit as the publicly funded public service broadcaster, and all proposed services must be assessed across a variety of measures. The concept of a public good has become enshrined in many of the structures put in place to meet the requirement for accountability.

Editorial independence was a strong feature in most interviews, although the interviewees from the Indian public service broadcaster feel accountable to government, and feel it their duty to reflect, generally, government viewpoints. The issue of editorial independence from shareholders was little discussed, although some concerns were expressed when issues such as pluralism and media ownership were considered. But these subjects were not the focus of this research and occur in interviews as a by-product of the main discussion.

Regulatory oversight is thought to be a principal form of ensuring processes of accountability are in place and observed. A number of interviewees, in all the countries but especially in the UK, query how far the accountability of the regulators themselves goes. There is questioning of the way in which regulatory decisions are evaluated and about the way in which government supervises regulators (except in India, where a government department is the regulator). Although regulators who have to argue for their budgets feel that they are made to be thoroughly accountable, some of the processes are thought to be less than rigorous.

Looking to the future, a few interviewees argue that the 'specialness' of broadcasting is increasingly fragile. As new technologies provide greater ease of access to a wide range of media content, broadcasting as a means of blanket distribution lessens in importance. That time is not here, however, and most interviewees feel that some form of accountability should continue for social and financial reasons.

Accountability will continue to be financial – to the audience or user and to the shareholder. But accountability will also need to be to those who continue to hold responsibility more generally for society, such as parliament or regulators acting on their behalf. With this recognition is an awareness that the means by which this might be managed – or might be capable of being managed – would need to change. The developing media do not require the degree of mediation that broadcasting does, and the interactive technologies are able to speak directly with the individual.

Engagement with the public

A form of accountability, rather different from either the use of constitutional machinery or the value-for-money assessments represented by transactional relationships, is the discussion about programme (or 'media') content conducted between the public and the providers of content, broadcasters and some branches of new media. At one end of the scale is the treatment of individuals who wish to register complaints or grievances or simply offer opinions. We gained the sense that complainants are generally well treated, if not always dealt with as rapidly as the individual member of the public would like. It needs to be noted that an effective complaints system, whatever good it may do to a company's reputation, carries a cost to the provider. We noted that a number of organisations have appointed ombudsmen to give an independent response to complainants or scrutinise the response given to them by the company concerned.

During the period of our research, Ofcom, the British regulator, imposed some very heavy fines on UK broadcasters for breaches of its Code and we noted in the same period the imposition of similar fines by the FCC in the US on broadcasters accused of obscenity.

Consultations are frequent: the Australian regulator, ACMA, requires public consultations by its licensees before renewals can be confirmed. The British regulator, Ofcom, carries out an extensive programme of public consultations. In India future broadcasting regulation is being debated within a forum, including representatives from disparate sectors of Indian society.

In the US, such activity is more coordinated and we talked to representatives of lobbying groups which are, in general, more numerous and active than those in the other three countries. The theme of many of them is resistance to the dominance of commercial values in American broadcasting.

The public interest

The American trust in the efficacy of the market in providing programmes attracting large and generally satisfied audiences remains strong. By contrast, the share of the audience regularly won by public broadcasting is small. But many commercial stations in the US, as well as in the other three countries under study, provide examples of programme content which can fairly be described as serving the public interest. Their presence in the schedules arises from their commercial viability or from a calculation that, even if not actually money-making, they contribute to the station's reputation locally or nationally. However, as we were reminded more than once, water cannot be made to run uphill. Forms of intervention will be needed if the public interest is to be fully served.

In both Australia and India, there is a specific national interest to be served – the maintenance and solidification of a national identity. To an increasing extent, that may also be an objective within the UK as immigration and devolution continue. Some may sense a paradox in these dilemmas created in societies with national broadcasting systems while the US, with no substantial national broadcasting system, appears to have a lesser problem.

For the moment, however, it may be valuable to recall two passages from the conversations reported earlier: The first is Andrew Graham's rejection of self-interest as the sole motive for human actions. The second is Reed Hundt's assertion of a belief in society. They are both indispensable qualities if broadcasting, to use a general term for a variety of models, is to provide its communities with the added diversity which is at present either lacking or at risk. New media may fill in some of the shortfall, to use Robin Foster's preferred qualification of market-failure, but any completion of that process is still a considerable way into the future.

Regulation

The ending of spectrum scarcity has brought claims that, with it, comes the end of broadcasting regulation in many of its forms. That argument runs especially strongly in the case of commercial operators. They are now well-placed to reject a regulator's unwanted pressures of the kind experienced in both Australia and the UK, where specific content requirements were conditions of the operators' licences. In Australia, there are doubts about how long such conditions can endure, while in the UK, the regulator, Ofcom, has already relaxed the terms of its licences for public service broadcasters, confining its requirements to News and Current Affairs programmes.

Two casualties of that decision in the UK are the output of television programmes for children and the industry in Britain which provided them. The publicly funded BBC remains the sole public service broadcaster providing children's programmes unless or until an alternative source of public funding can be found to support a competitor. The competition, once ITV ceases its transmissions of children's programming in 2009, will consist of numerous channels heavily dependent on American-made programming, although some British production is presented. Critics, echoed in Australia and India, argue that these programmes are critical to the development of children's understanding of their national cultures, capable of capturing their interest and stimulating their imaginations more effectively than may happen in school. They can form a significant part of the development of national cohesion, a topic which was touched on in many of the interviews. The threat to the national culture grows as globalisation spreads.

There was agreement among many of those interviewed on the continuing need for impartiality and accuracy in the provision of News and Current Affairs, certainly on the publicly-funded channels, but arguably elsewhere in both traditional and new media. Some form of independent content-regulator oversight would appear to be a necessity if the public interest in broadcasting is to be sustained. The experience of the Hutton Inquiry in the UK suggests that invigilation of this kind, which requires detailed understanding of the industry as it develops and changes, should not be a routine concern of the courts.

Discussions about regulation of the media in a digitalised world led to discussions about the difficulty of regulation in any sort of traditional sense, that which derived from a time of limited spectrum and closed networks. New models of regulation were discussed – and are being tried in some countries. What was of interest is that regulation itself is felt, by most interviewees, to be necessary even in the fast evolving world of new technologies as it offers a framework of accountability to audiences and users. Prescriptive regulation is felt to be outmoded. However, in India, where regulation of the content of private, non-public service broadcasters has been loosely applied, this is now being challenged by the government.

The future

The nature of the relationship that service providers – of broadcasting or other methods of media content – have with their audiences and users is in a period of change, exaggerated by the move to digitalisation and an uncertainty about what it will bring. Mark Thompson, Director-General of the BBC, believed that the BBC now has an explicit transactional relationship with the public, but with households rather than individuals. The nature of that relationship has undergone a change of which the new Public Purposes are an expression:

> It can't any longer be just a kind of paternalistic equation where the public may not like it, but they are going to get it anyway. But the Public Purposes have got to feel relevant and useful to the public. So the core of my model is around that one simple relationship. In a complicated world, a simple idea – that people pool money together, in respect of which they get services which are socially and culturally useful.

More recently the Internet and new media have introduced a great variety of services with disparate and competitive propositions for the public. In all of the countries under study, it is the case that the Internet is being used variously for entertainment and the dissemination of information. Meanwhile, broadband and the other new media delivery services have largely extended accessibility to existing content. This is liable to further change as new styles of content are produced to fit the different media forms. Until the time that these new forms are sufficiently established to introduce genuine innovation and seek out creative risks to challenge the audience or user, the responsibility for pushing at the boundaries of creativity and originality continues to lie with the broadcasters, most importantly, given their ability to fund programming ventures beyond the scope of many commercial schedules. As we noted above, not everything which might fairly be described as public service content will disappear from the commercial channels. Some programming will have sufficient commercial value to justify its place in the schedules. Some may find a place for reasons of the prestige they bring with them. All, however, are at some risk to the commercial fortunes of their providers, whether these lie in falling revenues or are the consequence of takeovers which can produce drastic changes in the focus of services.

The capacity of broadcasting to provide a unifying factor – to act as the national glue or allow the nation to talk to itself not only as individuals, but as a community – ought not to be allowed to weaken. An essential corollary of this is the building and maintenance of the domestic production base. If it were to be neglected, there would be an increased risk of fraying to the binding that holds together national societies.

The elimination of spectrum scarcity, even if only as temporary as some interviewees have suggested, seriously restricts the range of sanctions available to government regulators. However, that some regulation should survive into the future is surely inevitable (or desirable), even if it extends little further than a licence-giving role under which the regulator can reasonably demand some assurance of good conduct from the licensee. It may be that accuracy and the right to privacy can be secured through the law, but recourse to law is costly and often protracted. In the range of offences where broadcasters sometimes can be at fault, a speedy resolution is often highly desirable. That might suggest a different solution of greater reliance on self- or co-regulation with an appellate function entrusted to the regulator and an ultimate appeal to judicial review. Forms of self-regulation are being tested in some of the countries in this study, but always within a legal framework.

What justification remains for more than a very limited pattern of regulation outside the activities of the public service broadcasters in the four countries under review? What does the public interest demand and why does it demand it when the press is under regulatory control no more demanding than it demands of itself? In much of the last century, the rise in the circulation of the popular press in all four countries has been marked by the growing concentration of ownership in fewer and fewer hands, accompanied more and more by a parallel movement in broadcasting. The survivors of these long marches to the exercise of great power in the media frequently exercise power over activities far removed from television, radio and new media. Governments show them great respect for their apparent ability to sway the results of elections. In consequence, legislators who may be called upon to determine many of the issues we have been discussing do not necessarily act with free hands, economically or politically. The manoeuvring of powerful forces sometimes goes unrecognised until it is over. Closer scrutiny of proposed takeovers would be one means of countering such changes while the current range of tools for accountability, if possible, should be extended and adapted, where needed, to the new media environments in which the same corporate forces are active.

For an overcrowded and increasingly under-resourced planet, globalisation poses many dilemmas whose resolution depends on much more than material calculations. If democratic societies are to retain their independence with their foundations strengthened, both old and new media have indispensable roles to play in increasing the understanding between nations, communities and individuals. That is the realisation of the ultimate public interest.

Appendix I

Australian Broadcasting Corporation Act, 1983: Section 6*

Charter of the Corporation

(1) The functions of the Corporation are:

  (a) to provide within Australia innovative and comprehensive broadcasting services of a high standard as part of the Australian broadcasting system consisting of national, commercial and public sectors and, without limiting the generality of the foregoing, to provide:

    (i) broadcasting programs that contribute to a sense of national identity and inform and entertain, and reflect the cultural diversity of, the Australian community; and

    (ii) broadcasting programs of an educational nature;

  (b) to transmit to countries outside Australia broadcasting programs of news, current affairs, entertainment and cultural enrichment that will:

    (i) encourage awareness of Australia and an international understanding of Australian attitudes on world affairs and

---

* All legislative material herein (Appendix 1 and Appendix 2) is reproduced by permission but do not purport to be the official or authorised versions. It is subject to Commonwealth of Australia copyright.

(ii) enable Australian citizens living or travelling outside Australia to obtain information about Australian affairs and Australian attitudes on world affairs; and

(c) to encourage and promote the musical, dramatic and other performing arts in Australia.

(2) In the provision by the Corporation of its broadcasting services within Australia:

(a) the Corporation shall take account of:

(i) the broadcasting services provided by the commercial and public sectors of the Australian broadcasting system;

(ii) the standards from time to time determined by the Australian Broadcasting Authority in respect of broadcasting services;

(iii) the responsibility of the Corporation as the provider of an independent national broadcasting service to provide a balance between broadcasting programs of wide appeal and specialized broadcasting programs;

(iv) The multicultural character of the Australian community; and

(v) in connection with the provision of broadcasting programs of an educational nature – the responsibilities of the States in relation to education; and

(b) the Corporation shall take all such measures, being measures consistent with the obligations of the Corporation under paragraph (a), as, in the opinion of the Board, will be conducive to the full development by the Corporation of suitable broadcasting programs.

(3) The functions of the Corporation under subsection (1) and the duties imposed on the Corporation under subsection (2) constitute the Charter of the Corporation.

(4) Nothing in this section shall be taken to impose on the Corporation a duty that is enforceable by proceedings in a court.

Appendix II

Special Broadcasting Services Act, 1991: Section 6

Charter of the Special Broadcasting Service

(1) The principal function of SBS is to provide multilingual and multicultural radio and television services that inform, educate and entertain all Australians and, in doing so, reflect Australia's multicultural society.

(2) SBS, in performing its principal function, must:

(a) contribute to meeting the telecommunications needs of Australia's multicultural society, including ethnic, Aboriginal and Torres Strait islander communities, and

(b) increase awareness of the contribution of a diversity of cultures to the continuing development of Australian society, and

(c) promote understanding and acceptance of the cultural, linguistic, and ethnic diversity of the Australian people; and

(d) contribute to the retention and continuing development of language, and other cultural skills, and

(e) as far as practicable, inform, educate and entertain Australians in their preferred languages, and

(f) make use of Australia's diverse creative resources; and

(g) contribute to the overall diversity of Australian television and radio services, particularly taking into account the contribution of the Australian Broadcasting Corporation and the community broadcasting sector; and

(h) contribute to extending the range of Australian television and radio services, and reflect the changing nature of Australian society, by presenting many points of view and using innovative forms of expression.

Appendix III
Extract from Prasar Bharati Act, 1990*

Section 12

Functions and powers of the Corporation

(1) Subject to the provisions of this primary duty of this Corporation to organise and conduct public broadcasting services to inform, educate and entertain the public and the ensure a balanced development of broadcasting on radio and television.

(2) The Corporation shall, in the discharge of its functions, be guided by the following objectives, namely,

> upholding the unity and integrity of the country and the values enshrined in the Constitution,
>
> safeguarding the citizen's right to be informed freely, truthfully, and objectively on all matters of Public Interest, national or international, and presenting a fair and balanced flow of information including contrasting views without advocating any opinion or ideology of its own,
>
> paying special attention to the fields of education and spread of literacy, agriculture, rural development, environment, health and family welfare and science and technology,
>
> providing adequate coverage to the diverse cultures and languages of the various regions of the country by broadcasting appropriate programmes,

---

* http://mib.nic.in/

providing adequate coverage to sports and games so as to encourage healthy competition and the spirit of sportsmanship,

providing appropriate programmes keeping in view the special needs of the youth; informing and stimulating the national consciousness in regard to the status of and problems of women; promoting social justice and combating exploitation, inequality and such evils as untouchability and advancing the the welfare of the weaker sections of society; safeguarding the rights of the working classes and advancing their welfare; serving the rural and weaker sections of the people and those residing in border regions, backward or remote areas;

providing suitable programmes keeping in view the special needs of the minorities ands tribal communities;

taking special steps to protect the interests of children, the blind, the aged, the handicapped and other vulnerable sections of the people;

promoting national integration by broadcasting in a manner that facilitates communication in the languages in India; and facilitating the distribution of regional broadcasting services in every State in the language of that State:

providing comprehensive broadcast coverage through the choice of appropriate technology and the best utilisation of the broadcast frequencies available and ensuring high quality reception;

promoting research and development activities in order to ensure that radio and television broadcast technology are constantly updated: and expanding broadcasting facilities by establishing different channels of transmission ar various levels.

Appendix IV
The UK Communications Act, 2003: Section 264 (6)*

A manner of fulfilling the purposes of public service television broadcasting in the United Kingdom is compatible with this section if it ensures:

(a) that the relevant services (taken together) comprise a public service for the dissemination of information and for the provision of education and entertainment;

(b) that cultural activity in the United Kingdom and its diversity, are reflected, supported and stimulated by the representations of those services (taken together) of drama, comedy and music, by the inclusion of feature films in those services and by the treatment of other visual and performing arts;

(c) that those services (taken together) provide, to the extent that is appropriate for facilitating civic understanding and fair and well-informed debate on news and current affairs, a comprehensive and authoritative coverage of new and current affairs in, and in the different parts of, the United Kingdom and from around the world;

(d) that those services (taken together) satisfy a wide range of different sporting and other leisure interests;

(e) that those services (taken together) include to what appears to OFCOM to be a suitable quantity and range of programmes on Educational matters, of programmes of an educational nature And of other programmes of educative value

---

* This section is reproduced under the terms of Crown Copyright Policy Guidance issued by HMSO.

(f) that those services (taken together) include what appears to OFCOM to be a suitable quantity and range of programmes dealing with each of the following, science, religion, and other beliefs, social issues, matters of international significance or matters of specialist interest;

(g) that the programmes included in those services that deal with religion and other beliefs include:-

(i) programmes providing news and other information about different religions and other beliefs;

(ii) programmes about the history of different religions and other beliefs, and

(iii) programme showing acts of worship and other ceremonies and practices (including some showing acts of worship and other ceremonies in their entirety):

(iv) that those services (taken together) include what appears to OFCOM to be a suitable quantity and range of high quality and original programming for children and young people:

(h) that those services (taken together) include what appears to OFCOM to be a suitable quantity of programmes that reflect the lives and concerns of different communities and cultural interests and traditions within the United Kingdom and locally in parts of the United Kindom;

(i) that those services (taken together), so far as they include programmes made in the United Kingdom, include what appears to OFCOM to be an appropriate range and proportion of programmes made outside the M25 area.*

---

* The London ring-road.

Appendix V
List of Interviewees*

Marcellus Alexander	Executive Vice President, Television	National Association of Broadcasters	US
Mark Armstrong	Director; Former Chair, ABC	Network Insight	Australia
Ed Baker	Professor of Law and Professor of Communication	University of Pennsylvania	US
Steven Barnett	Professor of Communications, Dept. of Journalism & Mass Communications	University of Westminster	UK
Georgina Born	Professor of Sociology, Anthropology and Music	Cambridge University	UK
Jenny Buckland	CEO	The Australian Children's Television Foundation	Australia

*All interviews were conducted in 2007; job titles pertain to the time of interview.

Bill Bush	Director of Public Policy; Former Special Adviser, DCMS	Premier League	UK
Bill Buzenberg	Executive Director	Center for Public Integrity	US
Paul Chadwick	Director of Editorial Policies	ABC	Australia
Himavat Chaud-huri	General Counsel	Star TV	India
Rick Chessen	Adviser to Commissioner Copps	FCC	US
Bridget Fair	Manager of Regulatory & Business Affairs	Seven Network	Australia
Robin Foster	Former Partner, Ofcom	Independent Adviser and member of the Government's Convergence Think Tank	UK
Tim Gardam	Principal	St Anne's College, University of Oxford	UK
Michael Getler	Ombudsman	PBS	US
Sagarika Ghose	News-anchor	CNN-IBN	India
Jock Given	Professor of Media and Communications	Swinburne Institute of Social Research, University of Melbourne	Australia
Michael Grade	Executive Chairman	ITV	UK
Dr Andrew Graham	Master	Balliol College, University of Oxford	UK
Murray Green	Director of Corporate Strategy & Governance	ABC	Australia

Jocelyn Hay	Chair	Voice of the Listener & Viewer	UK
Richard Hooper	Former Deputy Chair	Ofcom	UK
Reed Hundt	Former Chair	FCC	US
Ashok Jaikhani	Deputy Director General	Doordarshan	India
Rakesh Kacker	Former Adviser	Telecommunications Regulatory Authority of India	India
Professor Andrew Kenyon	Director	Centre for Media and Communications Law, University of Melbourne Law School	Australia
Nicholas Kroll	Director	BBC Trust	UK
Arvind Kumar	Director (BP & L)	Ministry of Information and Broadcasting	India
Baljit Singh Lalli	CEO	Prasar Bharati	India
Martin Le Jeune	Director, Former Head of Public Affairs, BSkyB	Open Road (consultancy)	UK
David Levy	Controller, Public Policy	BBC	UK
Sonia Livingstone	Professor of Social Psychology, Department of Media and Communications	London School of Economics	UK
Sunil Lulla	CEO	Times Now	India
Peter Lunt	Professor, School of Social Sciences and Law	Brunel University	UK

Lyn Maddock	Deputy Chair	ACMA	Australia
Bruce Meagher	Director of Strategy and Communications	SBS	Australia
Rajiv Mehrotra	Managing Trustee	Public Service Broadcasting Trust	India
Barry Melville	General Manager	Community Broadcasters Association	Australia
Helen Normoyle	Head of Research	Ofcom	UK
Alison Preston	Senior Research Associate	Ofcom	UK
Monroe Price	Director, Centre for Global Communication Studies	Annenberg East, University of Pennsylvania	US
Tony Prosser	Professor of Public Law	Bristol University	UK
Andrew Ramsay	Director General, Creativity, Culture & Economy	Dept of Culture, Media and Sport	UK
Narayan Rao	CEO	NDTV	India
Lord Rees-Mogg	Former Vice-Chairman, BBC		UK
Debra Richards	CEO	Australian Subscription Radio and Television Association	Australia
Uday Sahay	Director, Information and Publicity	Government of Delhi	India
Andrew Schwartzman	President & CEO	Media Access Project	US
Ben Scott	Policy Director	Free Press	US

Jean Seaton	Professor of Communications and Media History	University of Westminster	UK
Andrew Stewart	Lawyer		Australia
Mary Stewart	Vice-President of Communications	WETA	US
Tim Suter	Former Partner, Ofcom	Independent Adviser	UK
Damian Tambini	Senior Lecturer	London School of Economics	UK
Mark Thompson	Director-General	BBC	UK
Jerianne Timmer-man	Legal and Regulatory Affairs	National Association of Broadcasters	US
Tim Toulmin	Director	Press Complaints Commission	UK
Sir Mark Tully	Former India Correspondent	BBC	UK
Penny Young	Head of Audiences	BBC Trust	UK

Index

Notes are indicated by "n"; e.g. le May, Craig, 76n